A Woman's
Courage

A Woman's Courage

THE INSPIRATIONAL STORY OF
THE WOMAN BEHIND ANN SUMMERS

Jacqueline Gold

EBURY
PRESS

1 3 5 7 9 10 8 6 4 2

Published in 2007 by Ebury Press, an imprint of Ebury Publishing

Ebury Publishing is a division of the Random House Group

The Random House Group Limited Reg. No. 954009

Addresses for companies within the Random House Group
can be found at

www.randomhouse.co.uk

A CIP catalogue record for this book is available from
the British Library

Mixed Sources
Product group from well-managed
forests and other controlled sources
www.fsc.org Cert no. TT-COC-2139
© 1996 Forest Stewardship Council

FSC

Printed and bound in Great Britain by Cox & Wyman Ltd,
Reading, Berkshire

ISBN 9780091914257

I dedicate this book to my beautiful sister, Vanessa.
Thank you for being my sister and my best friend and
for always being there for me.
Thank you most especially for your unconditional love.
I am so very proud of you.
My love for you is endless.

Contents

Acknowledgements

I would like to thank Lena Semaan who helped me to tell my story. It is a vulnerable feeling to open your heart and soul to a stranger, especially about something you have never shared with someone so intimately before. With your help I found the courage and a friend. Thank you also to Fiona, Hannah, Miranda and Charlotte and all at Ebury Press for your hard work and support.

There are too many members of my team to mention by name but I would like to thank all my staff for making Ann Summers possible. I would especially like to thank my immediate team; my amazing MD, Julie Harris, for your exceptional dedication and loyalty, my PA, Julia Tobias, for your relentless support, my publicist and agent, Ghislain Pascal, for your outstanding efficiency and professionalism, my make-up artist, Virginia, for making me look and feel fabulous, my driver, Brian Collins for all your hard work and my housekeeper, Linda Walshe, for being one in a million.

Thank you also to my wonderful friends, I love you all so very much; Dorothy for being my surrogate mum and always listening, Carole darling for your unwavering support and the way you always bring sunshine into my life, Sandie for unleashing the outrageous in me and for always making me laugh even when things have got me down, Val for allowing me to misbehave and also for the way you always drop everything to be there for me and Joanna – I am so sorry we didn't know each other for longer but you will always be my lucky star!

And finally, my deepest gratitude belongs to my family. Dad, I admire you and love you very much and Grandma, I will miss our girlie chats, your lovely warm smile and your zest for life. You are my inspiration!

Author's note

In some limited cases names of people, places, sequences or the detail of events have been changed solely to protect the privacy of others. For that same reason, they are omitted from the photo section.

CHAPTER ONE

Little girl lost

In retrospect, I can see I was the perfect candidate for child abuse. My mother didn't show me much love and her own self-imposed isolation effectively kept me away from other children; my sister was seven years younger which meant I had no one close to talk to and, since my parents had divorced, there was little contact with my father while I was growing up.

My abuser therefore had nobody in his way. My mother had not only made him part of our family; she had allowed him to take over and was herself helpless to resist him. He didn't just have the run of the house: he ran the house and everybody in it. From the age of twelve to fifteen he terrified me. I can't forget those years. And yet, the funny thing is, I can't remember very much of what happened before the abuse began. Perhaps the trauma of what followed has destroyed better memories. I really don't know.

*

My father, David Gold, grew up in serious poverty in the East End of London during the war. His childhood was about little more than survival. The conditions of the houses where the poor like him lived were cold and damp and his family had very little money, which meant food was scarce. Dad's father, Godfrey 'Goddy' Gold, was one of those East End wheeler-dealers who was always looking for a chance. He was married to the most wonderful woman, my grandma Rosie, who worked very hard to bring up her children single-handedly, as Goddy was either off womanising or in prison. She started by selling buttons and Christmas decorations at the front of her house and the young Gold brothers would help her out after school and at weekends. Her front room was later converted into a shop, called Rosie's Book Shop. The shop, which was located on Green Street in Upton Park, opposite West Ham Football Club, later went on to sell gifts, cards, sweets and football souvenirs.

My father began his working life as a bricklayer. At one point, he may have been on the verge of a career as a professional footballer. His father refused to give permission for him to sign up for West Ham, deciding instead that he should serve out his apprenticeship. So for four unhappy years Dad laid bricks and dreamed of football. He still managed to get on the pitch by playing football for 'boot money' (unofficial payments that players received in their boots) for West Ham, Fulham, Leyton and Barking. A premiership star Dad might not have been, but he was definitely a handy player: playing for London Youth against Glasgow Youth at Crystal Palace, he scored the winning goal, ten minutes before time. Dad never lost his love for football and, today, with his brother Ralph and their partner David Sullivan, owns Birmingham City Football Club.

When Dad finished his apprenticeship, his brother Ralph, who sold books and magazines, announced that he knew of a shop going under that they could take over. Dad saw an opportunity to start something, moved in and began selling books and magazines. As time went on, Dad, Uncle Ralph and Goddy set up several shops and businesses. I suppose you could call them diversified – basically they sold anything that turned a profit. Along with his two sons, Goddy began to do very well indeed, with the boys proving themselves to be natural business partners. This, however, was not to last. Dad fell out with his father in the late 1960s and the rift never healed. Apparently, my father did not agree with Goddy's strategic direction (if you can call it that), which largely meant that Goddy thought he could run the business on his own. Their business, which had just been named Gold Star Publications, was structured with nine shares – three for each of them. Goddy managed to trick Ralph into signing papers that effectively signed two of his own shares over to Goddy, making him the majority holder. Luckily, Dad and Ralph found out that the transfer was not legal; nonetheless Goddy's lack of principle upset Dad and they broke away from him.

Dad had met my mother, Beryl, through Mum's sister, Heather, and her boyfriend, now husband, Terry Green. They married and had me in July 1960. It wasn't until seven years later that my sister Vanessa arrived so I was on my own for quite a while. I now understand that my parents had problems in their marriage from very early on. I remember my mother was the dominant one in the relationship and generally got her way. She was a very beautiful woman, tall, slim and very flirtatious. She was also extremely insecure, nervous around people and, like her own father, frightened of her own shadow. In short, she was a mass of contradictions which, as you can imagine, did not make for domestic harmony. For example, if you saw her with my father, she was quite dominant: yet if she was unhappy, say, with the builders, she would go on and on at him but she wouldn't talk to the builders herself. Mum had no appetite for confrontation. And in complete contrast to the way in which she imposed limits on her children, she did things to excess. She smoked and drank heavily.

As for me, well, I was a funny little child – small, accident-prone, fussy about what I ate and very quiet. In those early years my mother was overprotective to the point of being dangerously stifling. Looking back now, her behaviour could well be described as paranoia. It really was completely over the top, with Mum becoming anxious whenever I went out the front door. I wasn't allowed in the front garden, let alone out in the street in case I got run over or kidnapped. Sometimes she would let me have friends back to tea but I was rarely allowed to go to their houses. That meant I virtually had no friends since they got fed up with me not being able to come over. I actually stopped asking Mum if I could go places. It just seemed to me that she would say no anyway and then I would have to bear even more disappointment. So I just internalised it all.

My mother was very distant. She cared for us and was concerned for our well-being and future as any mother would. She dressed me in lovely clothes and always made a big effort dressing me up for school fancy-dress competitions (which I usually won), but in emotional terms, I don't remember feeling any warmth from her and if she had any in her, it never showed. I don't recall any cuddles and I didn't feel loved but I am in no doubt she did love us, she just didn't know how to show it.

I was never allowed to go on school trips and even our family holidays were an ordeal. On the beach in Cornwall Mum made a point of drawing a fifteen-foot line in the sand around me – I wasn't allowed beyond that. Once again, I wasn't allowed to go and find other children to play with, but they could come to me. I can't remember if there were too many takers but I don't expect there were. After all, if you were a child and you saw this funny little girl sitting, looking lost, in a circle of sand next to her mother, would you want to come and play with her? Not likely.

We lived at Biggin Hill. It was a comfortable existence in a lovely house called Pine Crest which was located at the very end of an unmade private cul-de-sac. Biggin Hill is located at the highest point in Kent and our detached house sat on the edge of the hill looking over a large valley. At one time the views of rolling fields were spectacular. Over the years the valley has been built up by property developers and all you can see now are rows and rows of houses. The house I grew up in had lots of character and a pretty garden with several cherry trees, silver birches and climbing roses. Later on my father had a swimming pool put in.

The house was split-level so the front door was on a middle level along with three bedrooms. You would take another flight of steep stairs from the main landing down to the lower level and the kitchen, which was usually piled high with dirty dishes – that I suspect my mother might well have wished would magically disappear.

The lounge was decorated in Tudor style with oak beams, an impressive fireplace and a well-stocked bar. Materially, we were not short of anything. My father's hard work and business success meant we could afford to go abroad, but we didn't because Mum was scared of flying. We did manage one trip to America – by boat, which my father wasn't too happy about. It took five days each way and we all became very seasick. I doubt if he ever forgave her for putting everybody through it, but he was a gentle man and avoided arguing with her. I think he just wanted to keep the peace.

I am now convinced that my mother wasn't actually concerned on my behalf. Hers was neither a rational fear, nor was it just about my safety; it was more about her personal fear of life. I believe it was an unconscious concern about what would happen to her if anything happened to me. How would she feel? She seemed to have no relationship with the outside world – something that was to get worse as time went on. I think she would have been happy if she'd never had to leave the house. In fact, I vaguely recall her saying something to that effect at one point.

I doubt if she ever stopped to consider the effect her behaviour was having on me; frankly, I don't think she was capable of thinking beyond her own strange fears. Given the generally odd way in which my mother approached the world, I don't believe she meant anything malicious: I just think she didn't know any different. At the same time, I grew up in an era where the focus that exists today on nurturing children and promoting their self-esteem did not exist. In those days people seemed to be a lot more vocal with negative thoughts. I suspect that the members of that post-war generation probably thought they were being realistic and honest, and that there was absolutely nothing wrong with telling it how they saw it.

7

School was also problematic for me and I often faked illness to avoid going. Maybe it had something to do with my mother's bizarre protectiveness that meant, on some level, like her, I could not cope in the outside world. I was also painfully shy which naturally put me on the periphery of things. It's hardly surprising then that I was picked on by the other children who quickly saw me for the outsider that I was. I had very long hair pulled back tight into a ponytail that the other children used to pull. Mum never allowed me to wear my hair loose. I tried to draw it over my face because I was very conscious of my high forehead and my widow's peak. I desperately begged my mother to let me have a fringe which she finally let me try when I was nine. We went to the hairdresser's in Beckenham but the hairdresser told my mother that a fringe was impossible because of my hairline. I left without one. I also wore glasses, really ugly ones. To make matters worse, I had an eye patch over one lens to strengthen my weaker eye, which made me even more of a misfit. We used to play kiss-chase but nobody chased me.

School dinners were also a nightmare. I hate to admit it but I am very picky about my food. That's not because of any body disorder or anything; I'm just really wary of what's on my plate. One of the dinner ladies used to try and force-feed me vegetables which I then used to spit out. There was another one, a lovely lady called Dorothy, who tried to look after me. She was delightful and I felt very safe with her. Many years later fate would bring us back together when

I married her son, Tony. Today, despite being divorced from Tony, my relationship with Dorothy continues, as does my uneasy relationship with food. Friends often laugh at me when a waiter puts something in front of me, because apparently I tend to look at it very suspiciously, as though it might come alive or something. Now I tend to avoid overly fussy food and the restaurants that serve it.

What little respite I had from this lonely life came in the form of my cousins, Stephanie and Russell. Every Wednesday they would come to our house for dinner with my lovely Auntie Heather and Uncle Terry. That was the highlight of my week. While the grown-ups ate downstairs we'd be upstairs messing around like normal kids do. It was one of the only times I could really express myself and be the little girl I was supposed to be. Unfortunately, my aunt and uncle moved away when I was twelve, a move that was to coincide with the worst period in my life.

I don't remember much about my father at this time, apart from him being, as he still is, a softly spoken man. He was always working really hard so we didn't see much of him. He never raised a hand to me or Vanessa. I don't recall many arguments between my parents but there was definitely a lot of tension. As with all marriages, the reasons are not always clear-cut but apparently they didn't have much of a sex life, an inevitable result of not being able to communicate. Mum was often suspicious about Dad having affairs and I remember her checking his mileage on more than one occasion. Another time I remember being bundled into the car as she tried to follow him.

Mum didn't like doing things around the house and I'm quite sure that's one of the reasons I am an absolute stickler for a clean and tidy home. Cleaning was not one of her priorities and if it were left up to her, the house would have been a tip. So she employed a cleaner called Bobby who, as it turned out, happened to be rather light-fingered. Bobby was one of those people who would steal things almost without knowing it. She wasn't very secretive about it, either. One time she took one of Mum's coats from the cupboard in the hallway, put it on and left. She came back wearing it the next day and continued to do so after that. Mum didn't say anything about it and neither did she. Later on Mum and Bobby became close friends and set up an antiques stall together, selling all sorts of knick-knacks. She seemed to be one of the few people with whom Mum developed a friendship. Bobby had a son called John who had wanted to be a musician, but had never really made it and spent his time working in computers for a central London college. It wasn't long before Bobby introduced John and his wife Sue to my parents. They all used to have dinner together and seemed to get on very well. For a time John became Dad's best friend.

Life soon began to get very complicated. I'm not sure exactly when I became aware that Mum was having an affair with John but I must have been about twelve years old. Mum would pick me and Vanessa up from school in Hayes. On the way home, we would stop at John's place. He lived at Biggin Hill, in a bungalow on the main road with a back garden that had a very fierce slope. The garden itself was treacherous: from a concrete terrace there was a sheer drop of about ten feet. Beneath that, there was a mixture of broken bricks, glass, other rubble and stinging nettles. It was here that Mum would leave us, locked out of the house, while she and John got on with their affair for a few hours. With a front garden that led straight to the main road and a back garden in which two little girls could easily have come to serious harm, there was now absolutely no thought for our safety – a complete contrast to the way in which she used to watch over us. Mum was pleasing herself and that was all that mattered. We never went into the house and it was clear that we weren't allowed to. I was confused and lonely. Although my sister Vanessa was with me, our seven-year age gap meant that I very quickly got bored with her. After all, there are only so many mudpies you can make. I remember being so cold sometimes but I didn't complain.

While many teenage girls tend to appear rather older for their age, I was the opposite: I looked much younger and because I'd been kept away from the world and hadn't interacted with other children, my social development was not what it should have been. While the other girls were figuring out how to talk to boys and doing the usual teenage experiments with black nail polish and violent blue eyeshadow, I was living in a vacuum, away from it all. So I really don't understand how I figured out that Mum was having an affair with John, but I did.

One day my father came home from work and saw Mum and John having sex in our swimming pool. Apparently, he went back to work without saying anything. Most men faced with the realisation that their wife is making love to their best friend could be expected to react rather more visibly and even violently – but that didn't happen, perhaps because Dad realised it may have given him an opportunity to end the marriage.

What did happen after the swimming-pool episode is that Dad seemed to accept it; and from then on the four of them continued to meet up – except now Mum slept with John and Dad slept with John's wife, Sue. It was like some horrendous, cheap suburban fantasy. My father has since explained: 'I was in a loveless marriage but I didn't want to leave you girls. I was suddenly offered the opportunity to sleep with John's wife who was very young and attractive. I realised my wife had no intention of stopping the affair with John so it seemed to me to be the best of all options. I just went along with the situation.'

John would go into my parents' bedroom with Mum and Sue would sleep with Dad in the spare bedroom. As for me, well, I just got on with things as best I could. My upbringing had ensured that I was both introverted and conditioned not to question things. Vanessa was too young to know what was going on so we just went to our room and played as if nothing was happening. It was just the way things were.

The swapping continued for quite some time but, not surprisingly, it didn't work out happily ever after. For Dad and Sue it was always going to be a compromise situation. Sue was young and the relationship fizzled out. Not long after Dad started an affair with his father's secretary, Denise. This wasn't to last either. Dad was now deeply unhappy and it was inevitable that my parents would split up. He was very upset at having to leave us and conversations with him in recent years have revealed that he carried a lot of guilt with him. Much later, when he discovered that he had left us in the same house as a man who was to violate us in the worst possible way, it tore him apart.

I was absolutely devastated by the split. My schooling was affected and I had to stay down a year, putting me behind the others of my age which really hurt because I knew I wasn't stupid. In fact, it was around this time I began to take a huge interest in word puzzles of all kinds; not just completing them but making them up as well. I was so good at devising puzzles that my dad offered me the princely sum of 50p a puzzle to design them for the crossword magazines he was now producing which had titles like *Letter Fit* and *Easy Crosswords*. My father's move into publishing came as a progression from the book and magazine shops that he ran with his brother Ralph; creating magazines seemed a natural extension to selling them. I took my responsibility very seriously and particularly excelled at 'Find a Word', where you have to make a number of words out of one word or subject. I still love crosswords and puzzles, and feel obliged to issue the warning that I am a highly competitive, demonic Scrabble player.

The puzzles were a way of extricating myself, at least mentally, from the pain and confusion at home. I even worked on them during lessons because I wanted to earn money and be independent; it was a big incentive. It was also around this time that I finally found some friends at school. There was Michelle Yarrow, Beverley Dalton and Karen Carter. At the time I was probably closest to Karen, who always struck me as very grown-up so I looked up to her, and we both drooled over Donny Osmond and David Cassidy! Karen and the other girls seemed a lot older and self-aware. I had absolutely no dress sense at all and was still an ugly duckling: freckly, pasty and very skinny. Like many young girls I was a late developer, a fact that was not overlooked by my mother's new partner.

John's presence in the house completely changed things. We were all terrified of him. He had a fiery temper and would explode at the slightest provocation. When he came back from work we would all listen to how hard he threw his keys on the table so we could determine what mood he was in. Whenever Mum's friends or family unexpectedly visited, he would usually pour himself a whisky and disappear to his 'den' in a huge sulk. He sulked like no adult I've ever met – or child, for that matter. Dad would come over every Thursday night to see Vanessa and me, and we would sit and try to make conversation. It was very strained and John would again go off to his room. He was a heavy drinker and, under his influence, Mum also began to drink very heavily. She may have loved John, or thought she did, but it was not a healthy relationship. She was as much in fear of him as we were and he knocked all the confidence out of her. I was sorry for her and wanted so much for her to be happy.

John wasn't someone who engaged with people and that included me and Vanessa – he did, however, come up to the room we shared to kiss us goodnight. I didn't like him and didn't feel any affection for him so I just never reacted. Then one night when he came in, he put his tongue in my mouth; to be honest, I didn't understand what it meant. After he did it, he went straight out again. Now, having read about paedophiles, I believe it was the start of his 'grooming' of me. John knew exactly what he was doing. He could see that I was cut off both from my mother and the rest of the world. My mother was totally in awe of him so the field was clear for him to do as he wished.

The abuse built up over a period of time. He would make me feel special and boost my obviously fragile confidence by saying nice things to me. These were things I hadn't experienced before and didn't know if I was supposed to experience. I know that John was very affectionate to Vanessa but he didn't pay her as much attention as he did me. In fact, she only recalls him touching her on one occasion but he did take nude pictures of her. Looking back, I think that even though she was younger, John kept away from Vanessa because she was far more feisty than me which made her too much of a risk. Like any paedophile who studies his subject, John surmised that I wasn't going to tell a soul. I wanted to tell someone but I was also scared, not just of John, but my mother as well. My cousin, Russell, was one of the few people I tried to talk to about what was happening to me. Once when I was twelve, they were visiting and I told him, 'John gets fresh with me.' My mother overheard me and told me to stop telling lies.

I can't remember when things went from touching and kissing to more sinister abuse but one event really stands out. When I was thirteen my father paid for all of us – Mum, John, Vanessa and me – to go on a cruise to the Caribbean. He didn't have to do this but maybe it was his guilt. The list of destinations looked fabulous: Martinique, St Vincent and Barbados were all on the itinerary. I was so excited.

On the cruise ship one day, on the way to lunch, I started feeling ill so it was decided that I should go and rest. Halfway through the meal John left Mum and Vanessa and came to my cabin. I can't picture the specifics of that day but he undressed me and led me into the shower. He'd just let me come out when my mother turned up at the cabin door. John had locked it but Mum looked through the keyhole and saw him there with me. She banged loudly on the door. He unlocked it and, still pulling up his trousers, walked straight past her and out the door, saying nothing at all. Seeing me naked and dripping wet, my mother just walked up to me and slapped me across the face. She never confronted John but she did ignore me totally for the rest of the holiday.

After that incident I believe she knew exactly what was going on. The more I thought about it, the more I felt rejected by her and responsible for what was happening to me. I knew what John was doing wasn't right or normal and kept asking myself what I had done wrong. I was also living in a time when children did not discuss issues like abuse with other people. It was not commonly mentioned in the media as it is today and children were not warned to watch out for people who might be possible abusers. In fact, to all intents and purposes, it didn't exist. Even professionals were not very adept at handling it, as evidenced by my encounter with a female GP. I had gone to see her for my self-inflicted constipation. Over the years I had developed this habit of holding my bowels so that I didn't go to the toilet, at one point for two weeks. I was in a huge amount of pain. Psychologists would probably see it as a desperate child's attempt at gaining some foothold and control in the world and I suspect there is a great deal of truth in that.

I was scared of doctors but I was also aware I was alone with my GP for the first time. As she examined me, I suddenly blurted out something like, 'I'm being sexually abused at home.' Instead of making me feel comfortable and giving me the confidence to talk about it, she coldly asked, 'Shall I send round a social worker?' Hearing those words sounded so threatening I immediately said no, for fear of getting into or causing trouble. In those days the impression of the social worker was someone who took you away instead of helping you. After that episode and my childish attempt to tell my cousin, I kept the whole thing to myself. I couldn't tell my father, who had absolutely no idea what was going on – in fact, it's only recently that he has discovered what went on in that house.

John's abuse went beyond the sexual. He was one of those people who was menacing, even when he wasn't around. My mother became totally submissive to him. I won't say she was besotted in a loving way. He controlled her and she spent her whole life pleasing him, so Vanessa and I had to do the same. Mum's sole mission in life was how to keep John happy. He was not only her partner; he was also her main topic of conversation. She talked about him incessantly. When it wasn't about John, it was about his dog. And that was it: she had no other interests. John would often mock me, taking something I'd said and repeating it back to me as if I was stupid. Mum would then join in with him. His influence meant that she would put me down, often in front of people. I often remember hearing her say in front of visitors, 'Jacqueline's so plain and clumsy.'

As if the sexual and emotional abuse wasn't enough, there was also the 'work'. I don't mean picking up our clothes off the floor or tidying our rooms, but seriously hard labour. After we did our homework, we weren't allowed to watch TV or relax. We had to apply ourselves to one of four forms of work that John had decreed. One of these was housework, specifically cleaning. Often I would take on the worst room in the house, which was the kitchen. I don't know how Mum did it but she managed to make it filthy so I had to scrub it. There was no rest for anybody. My mother's chronic rheumatoid arthritis did not exempt her (although she had lighter jobs) and neither did Vanessa's age (she was only five when John came to live in our house). With John there were no excuses. He liked to have us working in the garden where he made us dig a vegetable patch. We'd be out there until it got dark trying to make inroads into the stubborn clay. Our work took place every day of the week; at the weekend we worked from the moment we got up until we went to bed. It was relentless. It also ruined our beautiful house that Dad had left us. Over the years John destroyed the look of the house and garden by chopping down the lovely cherry and birch trees and knocking down walls, replacing them with ugly outhouses and walls made of breeze blocks. He had no sense of style and seemed to do it for the sake of it. Our formerly beautiful house was now cold, untidy, unclean and generally neglected.

One of his favourite tasks for us was logging. Our garden led to a one-acre piece of woodland which my father had bought for my mother as an addition to the house. John would do the macho bits with the chainsaw and then it fell upon Vanessa and me to carry the logs to the living room. We had to carry them through the woods, across the lawn, up the steep hill, across the other lawn and inside. It was back-breaking work.

My other job was cleaning the swimming pool. The truth was they couldn't afford to maintain it so it would fall into a state of complete neglect. Then John would decide to empty it and I'd have to get into the pool with a scrubbing brush – a small one. I would scrub and scrub until my fingers were red raw and he would stand there waving the hose over it so the mildew would run off. The mildew meant that the surface of the pool was slippery. One day I slipped, banged my head and ended up with concussion. There was no sympathy from anybody. John was very annoyed with me and frustrated that I couldn't continue. My mother didn't care that we were working so hard. She just seemed to turn a blind eye. During the school holidays John would return from work (which he did not enjoy) and ask us to give a detailed report on what we'd done during the day. There was no respite.

During the summer he would insist we all sunbathed naked while in the garden and even fixed a device on the gate so he could tell if anyone entered. The thought of him watching and leering at us is one that revolts me to this very day. It is very menacing when you know someone's eyes are constantly on you. It is even more menacing when you know that he is going to sexually abuse you – but you don't know exactly when. The result was that I constantly lived in fear of him coming into my room. He was constantly following me, coming into the bathroom when I was there and watching me in the shower. He would engage in some form of sexual activity with me, on average, once a week and, during that time, did everything except penetrate me fully with his penis. He frequently went close to penetrating me but then stopped. Perhaps it was the fear of making me pregnant?

Some of my most desperate moments were when Mum left the house. My grandparents lived half an hour away and Mum would often go and look after them since my grandfather had had several strokes. If Grandad had a turn in the middle of the night, Mum would take Vanessa and leave me alone in the house with John. I knew what would happen. She would also take Vanessa with her when she went shopping. I would beg and plead with her to take me with them but she would just say, 'No you stay here and keep John happy. He likes you.' I think she knew what was happening but whether she used it to gain favour with

John, I don't know. He was a verbally violent person and they were constantly rowing. I don't think he hit her but on one occasion I saw him with his hands tightly around her throat leaning her across the staircase.

Mum hated it if John was not pleased. He used to have sulky moods that went on for days that I thought were weird for anyone, let alone an adult. He would go into his den and stay there and Mum would get very restless over this. Because he was nine years younger, she was always scared he would leave so she would constantly do things to make him happy. 'Make him a cup of tea and take it up to him,' she'd say. 'He likes you.' Those words make me shudder. He didn't like me. He didn't care about me. If he had, he would never have done what he did. All he cared about were his own perverse desires.

He never threatened us directly but his manner and the way my mother insisted that we had to pander to his every need made him a very scary figure indeed. To his own friends he was very popular, a good laugh and one of the boys but nobody ever knew what happened inside our house. The design of the house was somewhat unusual in that when you entered the front door, there was a large hallway with bedrooms and a bathroom leading off it. You would go downstairs from there to the lounge and kitchen. There was another staircase on the same level as the front door leading upstairs which you accessed through a wrought-iron gate. At the top of the stairs was my and

Vanessa's bedroom. When John came to live with Mum he bought a padlock and chain, and each night he chained the gate shut so we couldn't come out. I remember that at weekends we were sometimes not allowed out until 1pm. I'm not sure but I think Mum also chained it up sometimes.

I actually tried to run away from home twice. The first time I went to St Marks Church in Biggin Hill (where my mother's funeral was held in 2003) and hid there, crying, for hours. I then walked to the house of a school friend called Claire Firmin; Mum was called later that day by Claire's parents, and she came and picked me up. I didn't tell anyone why I'd done it. Another time I was about fifteen. At that point I had been moved to what used to be the study. John had been in there and put earth in my bed and my drawers, among my underwear and T-shirts. Apparently our dog, Kelly, had knocked John's cactus off the window ledge in his and Mum's bedroom. There were about ten plants in all that he had brought back from their holidays in Spain. When he found the fallen plants, he was very annoyed because I hadn't cleaned it up but his reaction was clearly not that of a normal person. I was very upset when I saw all the dirt in my things and just thought, 'My god, I have to get out of here.' I climbed out of my bedroom window, navigated the slippery eaves below, jumped to the ground and walked from Biggin Hill to my father's apartment in Croydon. It was a long walk in the middle of the night and I suppose I was lucky to be picked up on the way by police – who found me in Addington – and not by some weirdo. I told them I was going to my dad's so they took me there. Dad was packing to go on a skiing holiday in the next few hours. I couldn't tell him the truth although I wanted to and he just assumed it was because Mum was overprotective and strict. He drove me back and I climbed back up through the window and wrote about it in my diary. What I didn't know was that John read my diary. One day I came home and he'd nailed the windows shut.

Eventually, the serious sexual abuse stopped. One day I came downstairs on a Saturday afternoon. Mum had gone out shopping with Vanessa and I had been upstairs, physically shaking, thinking about what was going to happen. I never spoke to John even when he abused me which makes what I did that Saturday quite extraordinary. He was standing in the bar when I came downstairs. I said, 'This has got to stop.' Then I blurted out, 'It's not fair to Mum.'

Maybe I was cleverer than I thought I was because, in retrospect, I think I chose my words very carefully. I didn't want to inflame him or start a discussion. I wanted the conversation to end without confrontation and felt that appearing to care about someone else would help. I left the room, feeling worthless as I always did, and went back to my room in fear. From that day onwards he would watch me but he never touched me again. The worst was over but I was still not free. I started setting traps outside my bedroom door so I'd hear him coming up. He came in to look at me when I slept and still watched me in the shower. It was torture in the real sense of the word as I didn't actually know it would never happen again.

I would often fantasise about walking up to John, holding a gun to his head and shooting him. If I'm stressed, I still have these recurring dreams about him. And even though this may sound ridiculous, I don't think I could ever go out with anybody called John – the name haunts me.

CHAPTER TWO

Breaking free

If you've ever wondered why more sexually abused children don't speak out, I can tell you it's just not that simple. This is something that happens to you in your own house where you are supposed to be safe. You feel frightened, confused and, a lot of the time, you just feel very, very ashamed. I often wondered what I had done wrong, which I now know is a common feeling among abused children. The feeling of shame is one of the reasons you don't want to tell anybody. At the same time there may be people who suspect something is happening to you but they are too scared or don't know how to discuss it. So everybody stays quiet. It's like a silent contract.

On the rare occasions I did attempt to speak out I wasn't believed or taken seriously. Later on when I got married, I told my husband Tony about John. Although I didn't go into detail it was obvious what I meant, but all he could say was, 'I'm sure he didn't mean it.' Responses like that

constantly invalidated my feelings and made me very reti-
cent about discussing my past life. I didn't talk to my sister
about what had happened until we were adults and I didn't
seek professional help until after my mother died in 2003.
Up until then I dealt with it by stepping outside of myself
so that I was seeing it from the outside, somewhat
distanced from the reality. In later years, when recounting
it all, I would think of that young girl as a separate person
sitting next to me. That was my own way of surviving.

I am fortunate in that I am extremely self-motivated. If
faced with any problems, I always have an overwhelming
desire to help myself. Rather than wait to be rescued, I will
immediately start to look for solutions, believing that I can
overcome anything thrown at me. I also go out of my way
to avoid people who treat me like a victim. Of course, I am
vulnerable occasionally. Like everyone else, there are times
when I need the comfort and support of my friends and
family and when I am really hurting it can take time to get
through it. But there comes a time when I want to pick
myself up and look at what I have rather than focus on what
I haven't. I don't want to hear about the bad things in life
all the time. I am a very caring person and have lots of time
for my loved ones, and am there for them when they are
suffering, but I find it difficult to relate to people who
spend their whole life as victims, blaming everyone else for
life's misfortunes. I believe we are all responsible for our

own destinies: whatever befalls us, it is our own choice to become a victim or even to turn into the bully that perhaps once bullied you at school. In my case I didn't become either and for that I am immensely grateful.

Realising that my mum had probably played a part in allowing my abuser to keep doing what he did made it worse. Admittedly, she was powerless to do anything as she was completely controlled by him. But at the same time I think she used me as a bargaining chip since her biggest fear was that of John leaving. It was almost like she was saying to him, 'You won't want to ever leave, because look what you have here.'

Not long after my confrontation with John he did actually leave my mother for another woman and went back to live at his mother's house, which was within walking distance. Life was suddenly more peaceful and relaxed, but it wasn't to last. John had a cat called Eric which he took back with him but the cat kept coming back to our house. After about a year John's affair with the other woman ended and one day when he came back to pick up Eric it all started again with Mum. By now Vanessa was nine, and both of us knew this was bad news. Mum was relieved and happy. The inescapable truth is that she would have put up with anything because she could not bear being lonely. Mum's sister, Auntie Heather, pleaded with her not to take him back and my mum responded by saying, 'I know he's a bastard, but I can't bear being on my own.' Although John had returned, I was no longer subjected to him sexually abusing me; but since I had no idea it was over, the threat was still very much there. He would still watch me as he'd always done, his eyes incessantly following me. And there was still our punishing schedule of 'labour' to be done around the house.

Mum had been free of John for a year but rather than move on in life she had been paralysed by her loneliness. Of course, we all have moments of weakness when the familiar is tempting but I would never get into a relationship with anyone, old or new, simply because I couldn't bear to be alone. My life is so full of other things – friends, family, work, new challenges and so on – that I don't have a huge void to fill. I think this is largely a generation issue, though, as more and more women today give themselves permission to live the life they want, on their terms. Mum eventually married John on 3 July 1989. Apparently she told my auntie just before the wedding but only two people were invited. They were John's friend, Mac, and his wife, Vera. Mac was a friend of John's so Mum was able to have Vera as a friend. Despite the fact that Mum and John were now lawfully joined I have never called him my stepfather. I cannot and will not do it. He is not a 'father' of any sort. He was and will always be my abuser.

In my mid-teens I was still very young for my age, and my reserve and quietness didn't help. I don't think it was my natural personality but more likely the outcome of having led such a repressed life. For that reason it was perhaps far more difficult for me than it was for my peers to contemplate such a major step as moving out. However, while I didn't possess the self-awareness of a typical girl of my age, I had ambition and was very driven. I was a hard worker and more than anything I wanted financial independence. Money was tight at home, and although my father was fairly well off I would never have asked him for money. During the year in which John had left us, Mum had finally allowed me to leave the confines of the house so I could get a part-time job after school. I worked at the Beauty Box, a hairdressers in Biggin Hill, where I washed hair and swept the floors. The customers were mainly the 'blue-rinse' set and I didn't really enjoy the atmosphere. I especially disliked the woman who ran it. The only reason I'd got the job there was because she knew my dad so it was a bit of a double-edged sword. After my stint in hairdressing, I worked as a waitress at the Spinning Wheel restaurant in Westerham, where, although I worked hard, I was quite useless and finally left before I could be fired. I then briefly worked at the Flying Club at Biggin Hill, making sandwiches.

Work, however humble, presented an opportunity to be part of the world, something that had been closed off to me for so long. It not only gave me a taste of financial independence but also a chance at self-expression. I know that many people would not associate a job with *freedom* but for me that's exactly what it represented. Later on I went to work for Royal Doulton in their concession at what is now the Primark store in Bromley. I worked on Saturdays and during the school holidays, joining them full-time after I left school. I knew it wasn't going to be something I would do for ever, but it was a start. I'd always enjoyed art at school and for a while I toyed with the idea of being a window dresser, but it didn't really fit my vision of total independence and ambition. I'd read about all sorts of successful people and was determined to make something of my life. Staying at school was not an option, not because I wasn't intelligent enough – I believe I was – but because the environment at home made me far too unsettled to make a go of it.

Of course, one of the bonuses of going out to work was meeting people. A girl called Rachel, who I knew through the Beauty Box, introduced me to my first real boyfriend, Adam. He really was a teenage girl's delight: 6 feet 2 inches tall, blond hair and bright blue eyes. He worked at the local airfield as a lathe operator and seemed very grown-up to me. Well, he *was* seventeen! It was all terribly coy at first, with Rachel telling him how much I fancied him, then setting up a date for us at the Flying Club in Biggin Hill which my father owned. I wore a blue corduroy skirt and white halter-neck top with red and blue stripes – which sounds a bit like some small-town cheerleader's outfit, but at the time I reckoned I'd got it right! He danced me off my feet at the disco and I thought I was in love. Thinking back, I have to wonder what he saw in me. I had no confidence, no personality and definitely no style.

We ended up dating for almost a year, if you can call it that, since Mum said he could come to the house but I was rarely allowed to go anywhere with him. One day we fell asleep on my bed and my mother accused me of having sex. She didn't even wait to hear what I had to say but just started screaming at me. This was someone who, in all likelihood, knew that her partner had sexually abused me so her attitude really puzzled me. But then most things were a puzzle to me. I knew about things that no child should know about, and didn't know about things I should have been aware of.

Eventually I did have sex with Adam but it was anal sex. He explained that we had to do it that way because he had been cautioned by the police for having underage sex with his previous girlfriend who was only fifteen. (We'd been together several months when it happened and I was then sixteen, over the age of consent.) I realise that anal sex is not everyone's idea of a first sexual experience and it probably would have shocked me completely if I'd known more about sex. I'm also pretty sure I would have refused or been scared if I hadn't been abused as a child, but as it was I had no idea of what I was doing, or what was normal and what wasn't. Adam eventually found more excitement in the arms of an older woman and unceremoniously dumped me.

My mother immediately came over all protective, was very angry with him and demanded that I return his Christmas present – a splendid bottle of Tramp perfume!

Everyone knew I was upset about Adam so Dad stepped in to organise a blind date for me with a boy called Martin Thomas who worked as a petrol-pump attendant. We were to go to the Biggin Hill Flying Club dinner dance and I was so excited because this really was a big occasion. I wore a pretty white dress, and Martin, who I thought looked like John Travolta, did not disappoint me. After the dinner dance we saw each other regularly and I often stayed at his house, which was not far away in Biggin Hill Valley. My mother didn't like him, though, and she made it very clear how she felt about us being together. One day as I was strolling up to the airfield where Martin worked part-time behind the bar at one of the flying clubs, a car pulled up beside me. Inside were Mum, my grandma Hunt – my mum's mum, and Vanessa. Mum jumped out and just started screaming at me. Apparently my grandma had picked up a pair of my jeans and some condoms had fallen out of the pocket. Mum didn't stop to think that they might be a good thing – she just went ballistic then drove off again at great speed.

Martin and I had a good relationship and we connected with each other in every way. After my strange sexual experience with Adam I was at last in a secure relationship where I could enjoy sex, and I made sure I did.

When we first had sex I remember it wasn't a conscious decision but the time just felt right. We were babysitting at the time for my younger cousins. I remember feeling a bit nervous although Martin didn't seem to be. He was very considerate and there were lots of cuddles afterwards.

Since finding out about the abuse, close friends have asked why it didn't affect my attitude towards sex and my response is simply that I wasn't going to be a victim: the abuse was not going to affect my life in any way. In any case, I did not view what John had done to me as sex in the same way as what I did with my boyfriend. Perhaps it was my ability to distance myself and even to pretend that I had left that person behind but I did not equate the loving, fun, enjoyable moments with Martin as being on a par with the cruelty and abuse that John inflicted upon me as a young girl.

Eighteen months into our relationship Martin and I were engaged. The interesting thing here is that there wasn't really any discussion about what it meant. It just seemed like the logical next thing to do. If I am being truthful, I probably wasn't thinking beyond having a big party at the Biggin Hill Flying Club. By this point, Mum seemed fine with it all but Dad was busy trying to persuade me not to get married. He thought that marriage at such a young age would be a disaster and that I would finish up stuck in the suburbs with five children and no life. Ultimately his intervention was not required because our cards were already stacked. Martin's mother was an alcoholic, who was often beaten up by her husband. One night we were walking home to Martin's house after a party and we had a huge row. He punched me in the face and I landed in the bushes in someone's garden. I ended the relationship then and there, a move which I now think shows that I was growing in confidence. Sure I've had my dramas but there are things that I will not accept at any cost and physical violence is one of them. Nobody should have to put up with it or excuse it.

I was now eighteen and getting more confident about meeting men. One night at the Sport Air Club in Biggin Hill I spotted this very handsome man so I went over to talk to him. I was still at school and he was older than me, very charismatic and good-looking. His name was Tony. He was ambitious, hard-working and already doing very well for himself. He worked for De Beers as a diamond buyer and had his own house in Rochester. He was definitely in the 'good catch' category and a complete contrast to either Adam or Martin. We immediately hit it off; in fact, he introduced me to his parents not long after we'd met. Tony's mum turned out to be Dorothy, the warm, caring dinner lady from Biggin Hill Primary School. I have to say it was very strange to see her again and we were both taken aback by the moment. Thankfully we didn't discuss my awkward schooldays although Dorothy and I did get around to it much later. I also got on well with Tony's father,

Derek. He was Anglo-Indian and reminded me of Omar Sharif and was the very model of a charming gentleman.

It was 1979. I wasn't interested in taking up the trainee manager position they'd just offered me at Royal Doulton. Instead I decided to ask my father if I could gain some work experience in his business, then known as Gold Star Publications. Dad's voice said yes but his body language suggested he wasn't too sure.

Gold Star was the publishing arm of the family business which also comprised Ann Summers, then just a couple of shops. Part of Gold Star's business was in top-shelf adult magazines, a business we have recently sold. I have never had a problem with them: my attitude is if you want it, buy it; if you don't, then don't buy it. There is absolutely no point wasting energy complaining about things you can avoid, whether it's magazines or television shows, something that some people seem to do. The late 1970s and early 1980s were interesting times at Gold Star because we were raided by police on average every eighteen months. Forget those dramatic sweeps you see on *The Bill* – these were distinctly less glamorous. In fact, they were rather pedestrian and boring, with our warehouse staff routinely helping the police load the magazines into the lorries. The expectation that these raids would happen meant that their cost to the business was actually factored into the budget.

When I joined Gold Star there were no privileges. I spent my days entering data on the computer for which I was paid £45 a week, less than the tea lady. It was evident that my father had not gone out of his way to make it easy for me. I didn't see him much either – perhaps once a week – and since we didn't really know each other it was very strained. I also recognised that he saw the job as a stop-gap for me. The environment felt cold, not just because I was new but there seemed to be no camaraderie or team spirit. In any case, I lacked the social skills to be able to integrate properly. One thing that did amuse me when I started working at Gold Star was the way in which outsiders regarded our companies. You would see people standing at the bus stop outside the head office at Whyteleafe, staring in as if they were expecting something seriously erotic to take place. We still get that at our Ann Summers head-quarters in Whyteleafe today. There'll be a telephone engineer furtively looking around, hoping (and I'm sure he is) that a scantily clad woman will waft past (in his dreams). More than likely he'll walk past boxes of our products or busy staff inputting orders.

Tony and I were still going out and I'd known him six months when he suggested I move in with him. I had no hesitation in saying yes. I loved him and I hated living at home so in my mind there was no question as to what I should do. When I announced my plans to Mum, she was not too receptive but that would soon change. While she would never have accepted me living with girlfriends or on my own, she somehow felt that living with a man was more valid than either of those options. I was so excited at the thought of creating my own little nest. My considerable collection of Royal Doulton china was just waiting for a good home. Tony's house had been furnished with random pieces of furniture from a house clearance. I didn't like it so we gathered it up and sold it at Rochester Market. It went so well that we took a stall for a few more weeks, stocking it with bric-a-brac from our respective parents' houses. It was my first experience of direct selling and I revelled in it.

As soon as I moved in I swung into full homemaking mode: I believe I even made curtains. I also discovered how women can easily make a rod for their own backs because I did it myself. I decorated the house, cooked lovely dinners, and when Tony asked if he could help I said no. Of course, if you keep doing that then after a while the offers of help tend to diminish, something I learnt the hard way. But I was young, still a teenager and out on my own in the world for the first time. And let's face it: my mother was not exactly the best role model when it came to carrying a flag for independence.

Having left home, I no longer had to see John, but in order to see my mother I would go to the house when he was at work. I would arrive and she would open the front door. She looked pleased to see me and had this innocent look on her face which made me want to hug her, but when I did her arms would just hang limply by her side as she was unable to show affection. We would go inside and downstairs to the lounge where we would sit. Mum would then make tea. I often visited her in my lunch hour and usually the phone would ring dead on 1pm while I was there. It was John. Instead of telling him she had her daughter with her and did not have much time with me, she would take the call from him while I sat there. Mum knew I didn't like John but she would inevitably use the entire hour to talk about him saying, 'I know you don't like John but...' It was almost as if the more she talked about him, the more chance she had of changing my mind. I was forever attempting to change the subject but it was impossible. On the way to her house I would try and think of what to chat about: because she cocooned herself in the house and had few friends, she had very little to converse about. Occasionally she'd come out with something about a neighbour, usually something tragic that had befallen them. John made it difficult for Mum to have friends; I remember that she did know two women, Valerie and Jasmine, whom she befriended when she worked as a receptionist at one of the flying clubs for a short while. She saw them a few times with John but he didn't seem to encourage it. At Mum's funeral Valerie was upset that he never told her Mum was ill. Mum couldn't even talk to Auntie Heather or Vanessa or I on the phone if she thought John was about to walk in. She would quickly hang up as he would go into a bad mood if he thought she wasn't giving him all of her attention. Christmas visits presented problems, especially for me, since I now spent most of the time avoiding him. Vanessa and I would go to see her and I would naturally want to leave before John turned up. Mum would beg me to stay. 'Don't go yet,' she'd say in a pleading voice, 'John will be home soon.' I used to have panic attacks about going there and was so happy to get back to my little haven with Tony.

A few months after we started living together, Tony was transferred to Antwerp for six months to work for De Beers there. I stayed on in the house in Rochester but went to see him once a month for the weekend. It was more like an expedition than a visit. I used to go up to London, take the train to Folkestone, the ferry to Ostend, change at Ghent and go on to Antwerp. The journeys took their toll, especially because it was usually during the night. He came home for the weekend only once in all that time. Tony was quite a possessive man and had made it clear he didn't want me going out while he was away. I had no intention of doing so since I was still in the first flush of love. Also I didn't really have any friends in the area whom I could call and meet up with. My childhood had seen to that.

Tony finally returned from Antwerp and we began to make wedding plans. I was absolutely convinced this was the real thing. I was marrying a man who not only loved me but who shared my ambition and desire to succeed. We set the date for 20 August 1980. Nothing less than a fairy-tale wedding would do and both of my parents were right behind me, with Mum helping arrange things and Dad paying for it all. I had a fairly classic, traditional dress from Pronuptia. Given that I had no real sense of fashion or what suited me, I have to say that I didn't do too badly. It could have been much worse! My sister Vanessa, now thirteen, was one of my bridesmaids; the others were my cousin Stephanie and my friend Stevie, a school friend who worked at Royal Doulton with me. We held a reception for about two hundred people at the Grasshopper restaurant in Westerham and drove off in a white Rolls-Royce – it was straight out of the pages of a magazine. It was such a beautiful day and nothing could wipe the smile off my face – until our honeymoon.

One of Tony's least appealing characteristics was that while he liked making money, he hated spending it. He'd done really well for himself in Antwerp but he certainly wasn't going to spend it on some luxurious hotel. He'd bought a second-hand cabin cruiser and had visions of us cruising the national waterways, which, frankly, horrified me. The cabin cruiser needed too much work so instead he decided we were going to France. My father stepped in and flew us to Perpignan in his twin-engine aircraft where we had a rendezvous with a friend of Tony's and his girlfriend with whom we would be sharing a tent. Yes, a tent. Aside from the general lack of romantic ambience, I argued with the girl the whole time; and I ended up getting sunstroke. It was a relief to go home and get back to work where things were about to get interesting.

Dad originally became involved with Ann Summers shops when he supplied them with books and magazines. Ann Summers was launched by a man-about-town called Kim Caborn-Waterfield, who had dated Diana Dors and, rumour has it, Princess Margaret. He once wrote a sex manual under an assumed name. And he came up with the idea of Ann Summers after seeing the success of a chain of sex shops in Germany. He employed a beautiful young woman called Annice Goodwin, who, unsurprisingly, happened to be his lover and who had changed her surname to Summers at his suggestion. Annice managed the first Ann Summers shop at Marble Arch in London's West End. Opening in September 1970, it attracted a huge media circus; this was soon followed by public outrage which got quite out of hand. In the Midlands mothers and clergy rallied against the possibility of a sex shop opening, while in Bristol there was an evangelical protest march. As the well-spoken figurehead for Ann Summers, Annice handled it all with style and soon became quite well known in the media.

Waterfield chose to keep a low profile and let her run the show. Although the shop was taking in around £4,000 a week, Waterfield led the lifestyle of someone much richer, with the result that he spent more than he made. It was not unheard of for him to land his helicopter in Hyde Park, grab the takings from the Marble Arch shop and fly off to the races for the day. He only managed to open one more shop, in Bristol, before things went wrong and Ann Summers went into voluntary liquidation.

Dad and Uncle Ralph were owed money by Waterfield and in November 1970 they decided to go see him at the Marble Arch shop to find out what the problem was. The amount they were owed was £450 but, despite the shop turning over good money, Waterfield did not have it. He was a very clever talker and he blamed his difficulties on the recent postal strike since much of his business came through mail order. Predictably, Dad and Ralph didn't see their money but they saw an opportunity: when the shops went into liquidation they bought them and the Ann Summers name for just £10,000. It was a very good deal, largely due to the scepticism and hesitation of other potential buyers who thought the business was a bit dodgy and didn't want to get their hands dirty. Dad and Ralph had taken a risk that others were not prepared to take. These days I recognise the same instinct in myself and I've often thought the Gold motto should be, 'We do business where others fear to tread.'

Annice was kept on for a time but soon fell out with my father, insisting that she knew how to run things and implementing all sorts of changes that just didn't work. She introduced luxury Janet Reger-style lingerie, failing to understand that the sex business at this time was still male-dominated and customers were more interested in the black and red baby-doll numbers. Eventually things became untenable and Annice left. She was last heard of as the widow of an American millionaire with homes in Italy, America and London.

Upon returning to work from my disastrous honeymoon, I found I'd been moved to Ann Summers mail order, where I worked alongside a delightful woman called Marlene Green. I liked the atmosphere there – it had a genuine buzz about it and was much friendlier than other departments. Initially my job had nothing to do with the products. I looked after the personal ads at the back of the magazines, which was mildly amusing. We asked those who posted with us to sign disclaimers so that we could weed out professional working girls. One day Chris Rogers and Ann Galea, who were party organisers from the Pippa Dee party plan company, came in to buy some of our products to sell at their parties. They wanted to sell Ann Summers lingerie alongside their own range of normal casual clothes, which were the kind you'd find in the high street. We agreed to supply them on a wholesale basis. I was impressed by their enthusiasm and was especially interested in the concept of party plan, so I asked if I could come to one of their parties. It was 1981 and it was to prove more than just an evening's entertainment.

There we were, a group of women gathered together in a small flat in Thamesmead, drinking wine and chatting. Once the Ann Summers items came out things really livened up. Sexy lingerie was passed around along with stories of sex lives and relationships. There were loads of laughs and the most amazing atmosphere created by women who were enjoying letting their hair down. I was introduced as the daughter of the man who owned Ann Summers, which led to the women not just asking loads of questions but also giving their suggestions. Fundamentally, they wanted to buy sexy underwear but they didn't feel comfortable going into sex shops to do it. They felt – quite rightly – that the whole business of sexual pleasure at that time was not female friendly, a view that was eventually to underpin my business strategy.

Party plan, originally thought up in the 1950s by Tupperware in the States, could be used to sell all sorts of things. There were few overheads and you had direct access to cash customers. Right there I made my mind up: I was going to hold my own parties. I went back to Tony buzzing with excitement and he had to listen to me talking non-stop about it. I don't think I had any idea of what it could become; I just knew party plan was potentially a very exciting move for Ann Summers. However, I realised that I had to do my homework so I decided I wouldn't tell anybody – other than Tony – until I'd done my research.

We didn't sell lingerie but started with ordinary, casual clothes which we bought in the East End's markets. Tony and I would haggle with the wholesalers in an attempt to get them to give us only a few of each item, instead of the usual hundred. We bought jumpers, skirts, dresses and jackets – in all I think we invested about £100. I started with parties at our house and then I persuaded others to let me hold parties at their homes. Given that I was still quite shy, it was a big deal for me to stand up in front of people and sell to them. But once I was up there in full flow, I loved it, and the more I did it, the more I became enthused about what I was doing. Tony and I now had a weekly routine which involved buying the clothes in London on Sunday and selling them through the week. I got a really good feel for the concept and then moved on to selling sexy underwear and a few toys. It was hugely popular and transformed the atmosphere at the parties.

However, I had more pressing things to attend to. Marlene was complaining about how snowed under she was with the extra administration from the Pippa Dee ladies. It was time to make my move and pitch my big idea to my father.

CHAPTER THREE

Yes, women do like sex

I have always felt that my father is a very eloquent spokesman on the subject of the sex industry, which is useful considering the number of times the media have given the business a hammering over the years. He once told a newspaper:

> You won't find any hard porn in our shops. There are no back rooms. Everything is on view at the front of the shop. We draw the line at pornography. The difficulty is that the line keeps moving and a publication which is acceptable today might not be acceptable tomorrow. We have always presented sex in a healthy and positive light, and we feel that both men and women should be given the freedom of choice to buy products that enhance their sex lives.

The truth was that the sex business was then biased in favour of men. There just weren't the opportunities for women to buy products to 'enhance' their lives. At the time the concept of sexual pleasure was something that seemed to exclude any idea of women as consumers. The message seemed to be, 'Ladies, you can be part of it but you can't take the lead.'

I was under no illusion that I had a job ahead of me in getting my dad to listen to my party plan idea. Our father–daughter relationship was an awkward one and he also kept his distance at work. One night I stayed late in the hope that he would be alone in the office he shared with another board member, David Tizzard. I waited and waited but David clearly wasn't going anywhere so I just went in and told them my idea – badly. I rambled on far too much, but somewhere along the line I managed to get the general thought across. I told them about the parties I'd already held, the potential demand from women and how it would expand our retail business. Halfway through my monologue, Dad stood up and looked at me thoughtfully for several seconds. Many years later he told me that it was a very special moment for him as he felt proud and realised then that I had the makings of a businesswoman. Eventually he suggested that I go away and think about it, and make a presentation to the board.

I had a week to pull it all together. I had no idea where to start so I just made notes until I thought I'd nailed what I had to say. Then I typed it up and practised reading it out several times in front of Tony who said it sounded good. Over the years I have discovered that I am quite a lateral thinker and problem solver; even my friends have pointed out I will not offer only one solution to their problem but usually two or three.

The day of the presentation dawned and my nerves were already working overtime. They were all sitting in the boardroom as I nervously stepped inside: Dad, Uncle Ralph, John Gibbins, David Tizzard, Ray Unadkat and Ron Coleman. My father told them I had an idea and I shakily took the floor with my two humble pieces of paper. I told them about the women I'd met. I described how we could take the product from our shop range and use the catalogues from the mail order side so that additional investment would be minimal. I explained how women would be recruited as party organisers and they would in turn recruit from among their guests, which would begin to expand the operation. There would be incentives all the way down the line.

Ron Coleman looked at me and then said, 'I don't care what you say, women aren't interested in sex.' I was stunned, particularly when nobody disagreed with him – not even Dad. Now, when you're faced with a statement like that you either allow yourself to be put off by it or you just ignore it and hold your line. I was the seller and I had to convince the board that I had something worth buying. Getting angry would not have helped my cause. My father was particularly tough on me. I know he did it because he didn't want to show any bias towards me. He was also anxious to make sure

I knew what I was doing. Dad now tells me that as he watched me he became very emotional inside and began to realise that even though he didn't have the son he thought he needed to succeed him, he now had me instead.

The board questioned me for about an hour and I realised how it must feel to be cross-examined in a courtroom. My emotions were more those of frustration than anything else. I believed strongly in the party plan concept and I just wanted others to see it. But right at that moment they weren't giving me too much to feel positive about.

Eventually, and much to my relief, I was dismissed from the board meeting. I returned to my office and the waiting began. The decision was slow in coming. It was only a couple of days but it may as well have been months. Finally I was informed that I had the board's approval to establish the party plan concept in line with my proposal, which meant using the existing facilities. They also agreed that I could place an advertisement in the *Evening Standard* once a week for one month to recruit women as party organisers. Depending on the response, the board would then review the position. I was over the moon. There was a huge task ahead but I'd taken the first step.

The *Evening Standard* had all sorts of restrictions on what it would accept in terms of wording. Even though I wanted female party organisers only I wasn't allowed to say that and I couldn't use the word 'erotic' so the lingerie became 'exotic' instead. The final wording went something like this:

PARTY ORGANISERS REQUIRED TO RUN ANN SUMMERS PARTIES SELLING EXOTIC LINGERIE FOR LADIES ONLY. EARN THIRTY TO FORTY POUNDS FOR AN EVENING'S WORK.

The ad appeared on a Wednesday in May 1981 and I was inundated with phone calls, which I answered myself. I have to admit that a fair few were from men, some asking for 'Ann' (Summers). In the end I managed to find twenty-five genuine applicants, whom I invited to a seminar the following week at The Strand Palace Hotel in London, something I did each week for a month. I attended the seminars with Chris and Ann who had given up Pippa Dee to become Ann Summers party organisers. I brought with me a starter kit which I made up with Chris and Ann's help. It featured our products including some of the sex toys and novelties. At the first seminar I was hardly able to stand up and face the audience, I was shaking so much. The women in the audience looked unsure which made it worse but I just tried to get on with it. After I spoke I showed everyone the product range and then made a point of speaking to each attendee individually. We made a note of those who appeared interested in taking things further so that I could go and see them in their homes.

Energised by what I saw as my mission to feminise the world of sexual pleasure, I threw myself into my work.

Meanwhile Tony was getting fed up with his own job at De Beers and was thinking of going off on a complete tangent and buying a local wine bar called the Hungry Toad. He was advised against the move by my father, who then suggested he come and work in one of our Ann Summers shops. We discussed it and decided it would suit him; he was very outgoing and extrovert, and would be good with customers. With that, Tony went swiftly from diamond sorter for one of the world's most prestigious companies to working in the sex industry. He was very good at his job but being part of my family's business was making him insecure. There was little doubt that he was striving to make a major impact on my father. The problem was that he wanted it so badly. He was constantly demanding to know when I thought he would be promoted and I would have to reassure him while concentrating on my own rapidly increasing workload.

At the time I regarded the shops as entirely separate entities from the party plan. They were nothing like the Ann Summers shops you see today but more like old-style sex shops in terms of both their stock and their customers. Their primary market was mostly the dirty-raincoat brigade as well as tourists and gay men. The shops did a roaring trade in nurses' uniforms and maids' outfits (large sizes!) among the cross dressers. Items like gags, whips, handcuffs, chains and masks were mostly sold to the pin-striped City boys as well as to judges, civil servants and politicians. Needless to say, these professional men were overly anxious to portray themselves as fine, upstanding citizens who did not really indulge in anything so sordid as sexual play. They were careful not to leave a paper trail, always paying in cash.

Despite the board's reservations about the party plan business, they were beginning to discover that women did actually like sex, with the result that the business developed very rapidly. In 1982 I set up a telephone orderline system and employed an eighteen-year-old girl to take the calls. (I wasn't much more than a girl myself at the time, being still only twenty-one.) At the same time I wanted to make our catalogues more female friendly. Instead of being erotic and playful, until now they had emphasised the seedier side of things. And they definitely did not feature enough underwear that women *themselves* wanted: as countless department stores will tell you after each Valentine's Day, there is a big difference between what women want to wear and what men want them to wear, with the result that the more flamboyant lingerie is often returned. Our own research at that time told us that men liked women in red but women *thought* they liked them in black. The women themselves really liked wearing white or pink – which just proves that something as basic as underwear is not that simple! We covered it by having most items in five standard colours: black, white, red, pink and blue.

At this stage I was using the infrastructure of Gold Star to support my side of the business but the truth was that we were already on to a good thing and would soon start paying our own way. In the first year we recruited more than six hundred party organisers and our first year's gross turnover was around £80,000. Of course, as it went on I couldn't run it all myself and was recruiting more staff to help. The company became an all-woman operation and the parties were only for women. Many of the men at Gold Star didn't understand it and if I'd asked them what French knickers were they wouldn't have known. As for the parties themselves, they are always hosted by women because we soon found out that women do not like buying things like vibrators when men are around. Our parties are a chance for women to escape their husbands, kids and careers; to forget being a mother or an accountant for a while and tap into another side of themselves. Just as we did on that night in Thamesmead, women enjoy getting together to discuss sex, swap anecdotes and generally relax in each other's company. Kerry Katona, Mel B, Daniella Westbrook and none other than Zara Phillips – daughter of Princess Anne – are just some of the well known women who've been to or held our parties.

The party plan side of the business has gone from strength to strength and today comprises 32 per cent of

Ann Summers' overall business, employing around seven thousand five hundred organisers. We are the largest party plan company in the UK. Many of our recruits have become very successful unit organisers, in charge of dozens of other ladies, and their efforts have my admiration and support. It is always a joy to watch these women brimming with pride and confidence as they pick up awards at our Annual Conference. They are often housewives and mothers who now have the financial independence they never dreamt of. Party organisers join Ann Summers and receive a Starter Kit, which means they can start earning money straight away. The hours are also totally flexible, allowing women to fit their work into their personal circumstances. Our ladies have many opportunities for recognition and reward. Over half of our unit organisers drive company cars and these range from a Ford Fiesta to top-of-the-range Mercedes and BMWs. The earning potential is limitless and the job fits perfectly around young mums. You have to reward your best performers, otherwise you lose them. It's as simple as that. So we have competitions and incentives every month with high-value prizes.

As anyone who has seen our catalogues will know, we have a lot of fun with our products. One of our most popular party items in the early days were penis mugs: they looked like a regular mug but inside was an attached china penis. When demand overtook supply and we kept running out of stock, Tony saw his chance to impress. He located someone with a kiln with a view to making little china penises. You can imagine how his request was met by a lot of potential suppliers. In addition there were all sorts of practical problems with making the penises. First they were too large so they could be seen peeping over the edge of the mug. Then they detached themselves when a hot drink was poured in, giving a whole new take on the term penile dysfunction. In the end we got it right.

Tony's insecurity from working for someone was eating away at him and following his success with the penis mugs, he saw his chance to become a supplier for Ann Summers. He knew that I was having trouble getting enough of the right type of lingerie so he decided he would set up his own manufacturing company. We were already using two fairly well-established companies but we were struggling to get enough supply at the right price. Tony saw an opportunity to help us and himself at the same time. I told him that if he could provide the goods we wanted at a cheaper rate than anybody else he would be given the orders. Lest anyone think that he might have had it easy, I should add that he had to deal directly with Ralph Gold, who is one of the toughest negotiators I have ever met. I learnt a lot from Ralph although I occasionally felt sorry for our suppliers. In fact, Ralph's ruthlessness put at least one of them out of business. This was long before we bought from the Far East. One of the most important elements of our business – or indeed most businesses – is making sure we have a balance between good quality and regular supply.

Always searching for opportunities to reach a wider audience, in August 1985 I set off for Bristol with Tony, a designer called Angela Bailey and some of my employees. We were going to set up a stand at the Woman's World Exhibition being held there. The exhibition comprised everything from cosmetics and bridal wear to household goods, and provided an excellent opportunity to promote ourselves in the West Country. Our stand was actually like a room you could walk into and was themed all in pink. We displayed our lingerie, and made a small private cubicle within the stand where our sex toys were displayed on a shelf. There was nothing too risqué, just some of our most popular vibrators. We made sure the room was organised so that nobody could just walk in, and we specified they had to be over eighteen.

My aim was primarily to promote the parties rather than actually sell anything from the stand. BBC Radio West came to interview us and while I hadn't had much experience with the media I thought it would be good publicity. I heard the interview played later that day and was pleased with the way it went. It had the desired effect: lots of people came to our stand to have a look around. Tony stood there handing out catalogues and everyone seemed really positive, with the exception of two visitors. They were plain-clothes police officers, who informed me that unless

I closed down the stand I would be arrested. The charge was – and I still find this ludicrous – running a sex shop without a license! I have to admit I was a bit scared but I was also annoyed. I did what I would continue to do years later when confronted with challenges: I stood my ground. I informed the senior officer that since I wasn't selling anything, this could not be classed as a sex shop. Therefore I did not need a license to be here. At the time I wasn't sure if I had the law on my side – I simply decided to bluff – but it turned out later that I did. Even today Ann Summers does not need a license since it is quite rightly not classified as a sex shop. The police officer retaliated by saying that he would return the next day to see if I had packed up the stand. If I hadn't, he would arrest me.

Tony, Angela and I shook our heads in disbelief as we watched them leave. At that point my bravado nearly deserted me and I was convinced that they were going to march me off to the cells. I needed to talk to someone who had been through it all before so I called my dad, who had been through it all with his magazines. He was wonderful as always and reassured me, saying that what happened next would probably be at the discretion of the police officer. My view was that I wasn't going to give in and I was quite prepared to be thrown in prison because I was technically right: I was not running a sex shop. After the euphoria of the morning, the gloss had now been taken off things a bit and we all went back to the hotel feeling dispirited and drained. Nonetheless I was ready for a fight! Next morning I arrived at our stand early. I kept an eye out all day for the police officers. They never returned and the stand was up all week.

This was just one of our many encounters with authorities. On one occasion we were contacted by one of our party organisers in Guernsey, who was having difficulty receiving her products as customs would only let the lingerie through. They confiscated all of the vibrators, whips and novelties and even a book called *All That Men Know About Women* which had nothing but blank pages. We asked customs to tell us what products they would accept but they wouldn't cooperate, so we had to find our own way round the problem: we changed the names of our products on the invoices. For instance, a vibrator which was listed as 'Bully Boy Vibrator' was simply changed to 'Prince'. It worked – no one was alerted to anything unusual on the invoice and we were able to send products without intervention. In my world there is always a way through.

Tony is, in many respects, an old-fashioned man. He was brought up in a Catholic family and it's fair to say his idea of marital bliss is a traditional one, with a wife at home looking after the children. He was insistent about us having children and piled on the pressure. I was not against the idea of a family but I've always felt the time has to be right. I don't believe in having children at any cost and right at that moment I was in my mid-twenties and trying to build a business. At the same time my confidence was growing and I felt that I was starting to discover who Jacqueline really was. It wasn't long before Tony's insecurity gave way to jealousy. He would get extremely tense and go into a sulk. Or he'd go the other way and get so worked up that he would fly off into a rage. All of this made it hard for me to celebrate my success and I reconciled myself to playing it down. Once you start doing that with your partner, then you really are in trouble because you're embarking on a course of behaviour where you're literally editing your life for them. Ultimately if you can't share your glory as well as your misery, it just won't work. You can't make another person feel more secure by undermining yourself. Tony was, and is, a good man and I've always said that he is the perfect husband in so many ways. But we were starting to drift apart and the chasm was getting wider by the day.

Despite Tony's moodiness, nothing could stop me feeling good about myself. I began to lose the weight I had carried for so long, first by paying attention to my diet, which was something that hadn't occurred to me before. I didn't do anything drastic: I just stopped eating whatever came to hand and ate more healthily. I also started attending aerobics classes four times a week, which helped. For the first time I started going to the hairdressers regularly. My whole appearance was now beginning to change. Over several months I lost two stone in weight, reaching eight stone which was not just more attractive but also much healthier for my height of 5 feet 2 inches. It also meant I could get into some of the clothes I had avoided wearing. I felt more confident but also younger and more spirited. Instead of the timid, shy girl he'd married, Tony was now living with a glamorous young businesswoman – but he didn't like it. I wasn't getting compliments from him but I was getting them from everyone else which just made things worse. I started to become seriously unhappy and lost interest in the relationship. I didn't want to play down my achievements anymore: I just wanted to get out there and live, and he was holding me back.

I did make an attempt to seek help through relationship counselling, which he agreed to come to. Deep down I realised that it was going to be almost impossible to resolve our situation: this wasn't just an obstacle in the marriage of two kindred spirits, this was about the fact that one of us was making a major life transition and was, in effect, becoming somebody completely different. There were three major issues between us, any one of which would have tested a relationship: Tony wanted a family more than anything; I was becoming a career girl with big dreams; and I had a new, unstoppable confidence.

In 1986 we moved to Chaldon to an old school house with an air raid shelter in the garden that was perfect for Tony to run his new business from. It was a really sweet, gorgeous house and we'd fallen in love with it. When I tell you it was called 'Willey Broom' you can see why there was no question we had to have it! The move seemed to give Tony extra impetus and he did his best to spoil me, but the relationship was beyond repair. He'd hoped that the new house and his foray into lingerie manufacturing would give us a fresh start but while it momentarily revved things up, it was never going to address the longer-term issues. Our relationship was slowly disintegrating and any measures we were taking just seemed to further highlight the deep divisions in the way we saw our lives. It hadn't helped that I'd had such a dysfunctional childhood that I married earlier than I should.

One evening in November 1988 we were invited to dinner at a friend's place in Sevenoaks and as I looked around at her cosy little flat, I began to envy her independence. I felt trapped and at that moment I knew I just wanted to break free and live my life again. Back home, we ended up having a big row and Tony went for a drive in his car to cool down. While he was gone I quickly packed a suitcase and went to my dad's for two weeks; Tony seemed to be on the phone every five minutes trying to persuade me to come back. I told him the marriage was over and that I loved him but I had outgrown the relationship. Both my loyalty to Tony and my perfectionist streak meant that my family had no idea we had any problems so it came as a shock to them. We had a good time – ten years in all – but I definitely think I married too young. Looking back, it feels as though I was the youngest twenty-year-old ever to get married. Tony remarried, has a family and is a wonderful husband and father. We remained friends and still meet up for lunch every now and then.

While I had loved Tony, our relationship was very much one that reflected the place I was in at the time. Back then I was a young, inexperienced girl who'd lived this stifled, traumatic life inside the walls of her own home. I had only stepped out into the world when I started part-time work and, compared to other fifteen- or sixteen-year-olds, did not have the normal range of experiences: I didn't know what it was like to socialise normally, let alone how to conduct a relationship. Tony was my Prince Charming: good-looking, hard working and stable, he also provided the most wonderful reason for me to escape my mother's house. Perhaps if I had been more streetwise and confident, I might have waited longer to get married. Or I might not have married at all. However, I have no regrets: it was an important time in my life. I outgrew the relationship and, although it was painful for both of us at the time, it could have been worse if I had not had the courage to understand what was going on. I think once you realise that things have irretrievably changed, anything else after that is pretending. You are being dishonest both to yourself and to the other person. I know it's easy to stay with something familiar and even to convince yourself that is what you really want because the thought of the world out there is terrifying. So is the thought of potentially hurting someone else. All I can say is that you will hurt them more if you stay with them under false pretences.

CHAPTER FOUR

My sister, my friend

After Tony and I split up in November 1988 all I wanted to do was live in my own flat, just like my friend in Sevenoaks. I found a new two-bedroom property in Croydon which cost £90,000. I lived there for two years and finally felt I was in charge and in control of my life. I had money, I had my own furniture and most importantly I now had the independence I had been seeking since childhood. I also had my sister, Vanessa. As children we were not as close as we might have been if there was perhaps only a three- or four-year age gap. Seven years between us meant that we had not really had the chance to establish any common ground. It was not until she was sixteen and I was twenty-three and married to Tony that we became friends. One day she came over to the house where Tony and I lived in Biggin Hill and something wonderful happened: we found each other.

She was standing with me in an upstairs bedroom while I sorted through bags of jumpers and clothes for some of the parties we were trying out at the time. I don't know why I did it but I suddenly asked her whether everything was all right at home. It started as a very awkward conversation with us both skirting around the taboo subject that we had never previously discussed. Neither of us spoke directly about the abuse we had suffered as children but enough was said for us to understand each other. It was one of those moments of recognition, where we both realised how important we were to each other and how we had so much in common, not just as sisters, but as people. We didn't need to spell it all out verbally: we just both instinctively knew we had a bond that could not be broken.

While I was working on this book, I asked her how she felt and she expressed the moment beautifully: 'For me that was the day that the age gap closed between us and I met and fell in love with my sister. In my mind that sealed our friendship forever – I was no longer alone.' But it was in that same conversation that Vanessa also told me how painful it was when I left home to be with Tony. Her description of it makes me cry.

One of my most painful early memories was the day you left home – I suppose I must have been about eleven – and although there may have been a build-up to the day you left, in my mind it seemed like one minute you were there and the next you were gone. I don't remember any big goodbye, any hugs or any words being spoken, just emptiness. I can't say we were particularly close at that time – I am sure the age gap must have felt huge which I am sure was normal for siblings but the devastation I felt still stays with me today and even while writing these words I am fighting back the tears.

I felt so alone at home. When you were there you were both company for me and a buffer against him. After you left all I remember is the constant tension in the house, the aggression, the fighting and the hard work. We have often discussed the fact that my being feisty probably protected me from any unwanted attention but I had no idea what you were going through at the time. There must be some basic instinct that you have as a child because I would do anything not to be left in the house with him on my own after you left. I also begged Mum not to leave me at home alone with him but more often than not she would.

Vanessa tells me that well before John had ever tried anything on with her she was instinctively aware that something wasn't right with him. There were the cuddles on the sofa but only when Mum wasn't there or the way he would creep up to the bedroom at the top of the house very quietly when she was getting undressed for bed. Like me, she had this constant feeling of dread when he was around. He cornered her one day in the pool shed at the bottom of the garden and this time it went beyond kisses. She says she can remember the smell of the chlorine that was stored in there, the tools on the shed wall and the way the light struggled to poke through the two small grimy windows on the left-hand side. She knew what he did was wrong. She just didn't know what to do about it.

When my marriage broke up Vanessa was there for me. Since then we have seen each other through joy, drama, sadness and some seriously fun times. Vanessa had enjoyed her time at school and followed it up with secretarial college. At one time she wanted to do something with aeroplanes. She often talked about being an air traffic controller or an airline pilot, a direction which she obviously picked up from my father's love of flying planes. At the same time she was always being told by friends how beautiful she was – she's blonde with large, almond eyes, gorgeous olive skin and a fantastic figure – and they suggested she should model, so she joined an agency and did this for a while. She also did some modelling for Ann Summers but it was not something she wanted to pursue in a major way. In 1983 she joined me in the business. She was looking for pocket money so I started her off in the post room and she soon became one of the operators on our orderline.

Vanessa moved around the company and was eventually reporting directly to me. There were times when she forgot we were in a business relationship and she would cross boundaries – as when she burst into my office unannounced to tell me she was angry about something, but then she was at that time only seventeen. She soon realised that this sort of behaviour wasn't appropriate for the office. Like me, she has worked in many different areas of the business including, marketing, design and buying and merchandising, which has given her a wealth of knowledge across the whole business. Vanessa has always shown great passion and commitment towards Ann Summers and in 2000 I was very proud to be able to promote her to Buying Director. She excels in many areas especially product development, which is critical to our business, and negotiating – thanks, to Vanessa, we now have one of the best margins on the high street. She is a great communicator at all levels which has been particularly valuable when dealing with councils. If you have members of your family working for you, you need to establish that a job in the business is an opportunity, rather than a birthright, and Vanessa has earned her position in the company.

When we're not working we both love getting dressed up and going out. We had both lived such a sheltered life that the times Vanessa came around to my house in Chaldon in the 1980s to go out were a major event in themselves. We would spend a lot of time getting ready, listening to music and chatting. In some ways the drive to the bar or club was the most exciting part – this was hardly surprising, given that the night out would consist of the two of us driving to the place, going in, ordering a soft drink and waiting on the side of the dance floor for either Taylor Dayne's 'Tell It To My Heart' or Womack & Womack's 'Teardrops' before leaving to go home! We still laugh about it to this day.

As our world has become bigger and we have expanded our social horizons, we've had some very amusing times. One of these happened at the Emporium nightclub in Leicester Square in the late 1990s. Vanessa and I were meeting our friend Anna-Marie and she'd invited us into the club's VIP area. As we entered we didn't realise that the bouncer needed to stamp our hand as proof of entry, so when we left our bags, coats and champagne to go and have a dance we were horrified to find on our return that he wouldn't let us back in. I tried to explain the situation in my normal business-like manner, but he was a typical 'jobsworth' with a serious power attitude and refused to even listen to what I had to say. Vanessa then went to the bar, hoping to find somebody more helpful. In my wisdom (and out of sheer desperation) I had taken a long run at the steps leading to the VIP area, hoping to dodge the six-foot bouncer. Vanessa says she has no idea what I thought I would achieve but I succeeded in being caught, lifted and manhandled to the dance floor with the words 'you are barred'. Vanessa could only look on with horror.

All was not lost. A few minutes later a smartly dressed gentleman appeared and asked what was wrong – on explaining our predicament, he clicked his fingers at the bouncer who begrudgingly let us back into the VIP area. The gentleman then invited us into another room, advising us that a prince from India wanted to have a drink with Vanessa. Out of curiosity we went into this private room, where a man was sitting on his own surrounded by an entourage of about twenty men. It was a unique experience but we soon got bored and Vanessa was desperately trying to think of a polite way to make our escape. She leant over to the prince and told him it was time to go as her sister had had a little too much to drink – he offered his driver to take us home but when she declined he stood up and said he would escort us to the front door. As she passed by me she told me to act drunk as this was our way of leaving. With that, the prince, Vanessa, his bodyguard and I made our way to the front of the club. In my haste I grabbed the banister which was an unfixed rope, lost my footing and fell down the stairs. Vanessa came to help me and whispered in my ear, 'I said act drunk, but not *that* drunk!'

I suppose it may be because of my professional position, but many people seem to think I am the sensible sister when, in truth, that title should belong to Vanessa (but I'm not supposed to say that). While I may be in control professionally, it is she who often takes charge socially. In 1998, when I was newly single, Vanessa and I were on our way to a bar in Croydon with a friend called Leigh. I was listening intently to the stories Leigh was telling us in the car, all about her one-night stands. At the time the concept of a one-night stand was unknown to me; I had never had one. Vanessa was watching me and told me later that she could already see this was a dangerous subject, given my new single status. When we got to the bar I was keen to continue the discussion but Vanessa, concerned that the discussion may lead to some sort of action, decided to step in. My dreams of a wild night of passion with a handsome stranger were quickly dashed as Vanessa said in her most sensible and slightly alarmed voice, 'Jacqueline ... *not* in Croydon!'

Our love of girlie nights of getting ready with loud music and a glass or two of rosé hasn't changed one bit over the years. These days we have a great group of girlfriends, a much wider love of music, loads more confidence and no longer seem to have problems getting onto the VIP list! As with all relationships, there are days where we are grumpy with each other, but they are few. We see each other almost every day – our offices are next door to each other and there will always be time for a quick catch up at least once during the day as we both attend to our various meetings and commitments. We have dinner at least once a week with Dad and often again on our own. Then there are the shopping trips – we are both girlie girls and love fashion. We also adore time with our girlfriends, pink champagne and plenty of good-looking, male attention. While I am known by family and friends as a 'fixer' and will not give up until a problem is solved, Vanessa is wise beyond her years and the advice she gives is sound and sensible. And she is also a great storyteller, just like our father.

She is unbelievably protective of me and will drop anything if I need her. Although I now live about fifteen minutes from her, she used to live exactly one mile away, door to door, close enough for me to call on her when I needed her help. She has often been called late at night to deal with a gigantic spider that had broken through the window, run up my stairs and placed itself in an aggressive manner near my bed. She would arrive to find me standing frozen with fear on the bed, waiting for her to wrestle with the spider and save me.

CHAPTER FIVE

Dancing with drugs

Not too many businesses can justify having a troupe of dancers, but we can. One of the joys of a company like Ann Summers is that there are so many opportunities for innovative marketing. The idea of having a Roadshow originated in 1987 when one of our party organisers created a fashion show with a few girls and guys she knew. Wearing Ann Summers outfits, they danced in nightclubs while she canvassed both party bookings and recruits. One night some of my area managers invited me along to one of these shows, in Uxbridge, Middlesex. While the dancers were all pretty sexy, one of the male dancers caught my eye – he was just gorgeous with an amazing body. His name was Ben. He was twenty-four, four years my junior and once we got talking I found out he was confident and intelligent, which just made him even more attractive. In all, he was quite a package and I really fancied him.

By 1988 the dancers had been reinvented as the Ann Summers Xperience and were playing to delighted audiences abroad as well as in Britain. Working on the premise that you can never have too much of a good thing, we launched another dance group, Xcalibur, five years later which Ben would eventually join. While Xperience had both girls and guys who danced raunchily, Xcalibur was an all-male group, more along the lines of the Chippendales. I can't tell you how difficult it was to find five men who looked delicious, could dance and were happy removing their clothes. Never being one to shirk a challenge, I searched high and low, initially seeking out an existing dance group with a view to training them. That didn't work so we were at a bit of a loss, when Vanessa and I had a chance meeting with a blond Adonis called Steve Golding. Of all the places in the world, we found him in a wine bar in Croydon! He had modelled but was finding times a bit lean and was definitely open to new things. A meeting was set and that was how, one very pleasant day, Steve turned up at our offices with four tanned, trim and gorgeous men. Now all we had to do was turn them into a hot and disciplined dance troupe. It took a bit of work but they became a huge success – it's amazing the effect a group of men in G-strings can have on an audience of women. Unfortunately, the women can get a bit overexcited, with some of the dancers suffering scratches and bruising, as well as having their underwear torn off in the heat of the moment.

Tony and I were still in the throes of separation when I met Ben so for a while things were just kept simmering at friendship level, but there was no doubt we were both very interested. I went to watch more shows, which meant we began to see each other more often, until a few months later in 1988 we began a relationship. It was Ben who made the first move, something which appeals to a certain old-fashioned side of me. He was an electrician by day and a dancer by night and we got on very well, even though his lifestyle was very different to mine. We became inseparable very quickly – within the limits of my work schedule and his shows! We went out a lot to nightclubs and parties; we went on holidays and we led a very busy social life. It was a complete contrast to my previous relationships.

Ben represented a new, expansive phase in my life. When he came along it was as if he'd tapped into something that was already in me: a desire to get out there and discover the world, to meet new people and open my mind to new experiences. I was already going places as a young businesswoman and now I wanted to do the same in my personal life. When we were together it was always fun and incredibly exciting. So was the sex: when we first met we were having sex up to six times a day. I hadn't had anything like that and I soon discovered why. Apparently before he met me he'd been taking steroids to give him the body he wanted. But they had also impaired his sex drive. By the time we got together he'd started taking testosterone to counteract their effect. He went through a transition phase while the testosterone was working and eventually his body found what I suppose was its natural level. But even when things cooled down and we weren't having sex six times a day, it was still pretty frequent and it was wonderful.

Like Tony, Ben was ambitious. He'd mentioned a few times that he didn't want to be an electrician all his life. So when I casually suggested that he'd make a great salesman, he jumped at the idea and almost immediately began to look for a sales position. Initially, the recruitment agencies weren't interested in him because of his lack of experience, but then one came back with a job offer which would be based in the City. Ben was really excited and applied. We were about to go to Tenerife for a week's holiday so the agency made an interview appointment for his return. He was absolutely overflowing with confidence and was sure the job was his. When we got back from holiday things had changed, and the position had been taken while he was away. Poor Ben! He had bought a new suit especially and had mentally prepared himself. I didn't know what to say. On the day of the interview he suddenly went and put his suit on, saying he was going to go to it anyway, and would pretend he was unaware the job had now been taken. He duly went off and was seen. They asked him loads of questions, gave him the usual psychometric tests and he got the job. That was typical of Ben's attitude and it was hard not to admire him, particularly as he had a mortgage and he was taking a risk stepping outside his comfort zone.

I really respect people who take calculated risks, whether it's personally or in business. How many people are out there now thinking they want to change their jobs, move to the country or go back to study but haven't got the courage and determination to do it? It's very easy to talk about an idea – anyone can do that – but just having it does not make you clever. The people who have the guts to act on their ideas win my admiration. You generally won't find them saying things like, 'I'll do it in a couple of years, I haven't got the money now or it's not the right time.' The truth is that there is hardly ever a 'right time' – it's up to you to decide that the time is right for you. If you find yourself in a situation where you're worrying what will happen if you do take a particular course of action, why not ask yourself instead, 'What will happen if I don't?' The alternative is to end up being one of those people who thought about it but never did it.

Ben took to his new life in sales like a duck to water, working in the City for a year before he was transferred to Reigate. Though he was also still dancing with Xperience by night, we nevertheless managed to have a fantastic relationship with a surprisingly good social life. I often think the more you do, the more you can fit in and that was certainly the case with us. We worked hard and played hard. The fact that he was also one of our dancers didn't cause him any problem, partly I think because he wasn't directly responsible to me and partly because, unlike Tony, he seemed not to suffer any insecurities associated with my success. I found that refreshing because I could just go ahead and be me.

The dancers are a big attraction at our Annual Conference, which they usually open. In 1992 one of my staff suggested that it would have even more impact if the Managing Director were to join the act and that is how I came to find myself in a dance studio in Fulham getting hot and sweaty with a group of hunky men, including my boyfriend. You have to remember I was still a fairly reserved person back then who was concentrating on running a business, so this was very out of character. We took it extremely seriously and practised for months beforehand. It felt like I was preparing for the TV series *Faking It*, where they take people from one occupation and teach them a totally different one. Ben was brilliant about it all and very comfortable with the idea. The rest of the troupe were somewhat bemused at having their normally groomed and suited boss cavorting about with them and I was terrified of making a fool of myself. However, on the day of the performance, once the music started I suddenly just clicked into the routine and when the audience began applauding me, it just made me want to go for it. Situations in which executives step outside their usual role and try and be 'one of the people' can often be seen as gimmicky. Sometimes it can even backfire on them, leaving them looking silly. In this case, it worked brilliantly because it was totally appropriate to the culture of our business and completely unexpected.

I may have been in charge of a thriving company but I was still naïve about life in so many respects. It was at least a few years after meeting Ben that I realised he was doing drugs. I had never encountered the drug culture – I didn't even smoke cigarettes – so being with someone to whom it became a daily ritual was a major shock. I didn't initially understand how Ben could be a great salesman by day (he was very good) and dance at night. Now I know he was doing speed. Later on it became cocaine and then all sorts of other things. However, at the time I was in love with him and, even if I had known from the beginning, I suspect that I would have accepted it as I am not a judgemental person. I would equally have been naïve enough to not realise the negative impact it would later have on our relationship.

I'm pretty convinced that initially he was doing drugs purely as a social thing. He never pressured me to take anything, but several years after we met I found out that in the first week of dating each other he'd spiked my drink with speed. He'd taken me to a nightclub in Uxbridge called Queens and put the stuff in my drink while I was in the toilets. I don't know whether he thought it was amusing or if he felt that I was more likely to be on his wavelength if I was also on his drugs. Apparently I came back from the toilet and commented how fizzy my Coke was.

I am somebody who will try things once and as the relationship progressed, I did knowingly try speed. Rather than it being a whimsical decision or one taken under the influence of alcohol, it was actually quite measured. I simply wanted to see what it was like to be in his world. I didn't try much: it did little for me and I hated the way I felt the next morning. I thought it was hugely overrated but then I am someone who gets very tipsy on just two glasses of wine! In later years he often took ecstasy, Viagra, cocaine and a sleeping pill in the same night. He called it his toolkit and often commented that if he took it in the wrong order he would wake up on the dance floor with a hard on! It was actually to happen at a place called Joe Bananas, after we'd finally split up. I heard he'd taken the sleeping pill instead of the ecstasy tablet and passed out on the dance floor. By this point he was edging towards seventeen stone and his unfortunate friends had to lift this dead weight up the staircase.

The drugs didn't affect things too much in those early years (well, not that I could tell) and we had the most wonderful time together. I felt like I'd been set free and bit by bit I was becoming less shy and much more comfortable in my own skin. In January 1993, Dominic O'Shea who photographed our catalogue and was a good friend of Vanessa's, offered to shoot a private photo session for Vanessa and me. The idea was that we'd have sexy pictures taken for our boyfriends. Dominic was an excellent photographer and very patient with us, showing us how to pose. He had to instruct me far more than Vanessa. She had done some modelling of Ann Summers lingerie, but I wasn't used to being photographed with very little on (some of the photographs were semi-naked); however, I overcame my initial shyness and enjoyed the session very much. We were really pleased with the results and our boyfriends were absolutely delighted. Several months later Dominic had an accident on his motorbike and was rushed into hospital. It was pretty bad and he was unable to work for quite a while so he went away to convalesce – I was told it was Cuba – and we didn't hear from him until a few years later.

By 1994 things with Ben were not going so well. Increasingly I was being excluded from his after-hours existence, which was populated by dancers and others who kept equally strange hours. I had no desire to have drugs as part of my world, socially or otherwise, but they were beginning to dominate his and were definitely integral to his social life. Whether I liked it or not, they were becoming part of *my* life. I suppose I should have seen the warning signs then but we never do, do we? It's amazing what we will overlook when we are in love. Ben's entire personality was definitely addictive and he had a tendency to do everything to excess. When I first met him, he was a trim, taut, twelve stone in weight. When we finally split, almost ten years later, he had ballooned to seventeen stone. From being a healthy guy who preferred chicken and salad, he became someone who would raid the fridge at night for chocolate and biscuits. He also drank twice as fast as everyone else. This coincided with him taking steroids again which meant he became quite aggressive. I'll never forget going into the bathroom one time and putting my arms around him. He pushed me away and I was really shocked. It was one of those symbolic moments in a relationship that you don't forget. We had always been open and communicative so I asked him what was going on. He said, 'If you want me to have a body like this I have to take steroids which make me aggressive, so tough!' In other words, there was to be no discussion. My lovely, charming man was turning into something I didn't understand.

By now he was often coming in at around ten in the morning. Other women might have suspected an affair, but I didn't. I'll admit I was a bit too trusting then. It wasn't that I refused to see what was happening – I will always face up to reality – I was just too inexperienced to recognise the signs. He'd been less attentive, less interested in sharing things with me, showing me no affection and generally not treating me as well as I'd come to expect from him. I wasn't happy but I put it down to his work and too much socialising. Feeling neglected and in need of some recreation, I went out with Vanessa to a nightclub. There was a guy there who paid me a lot of attention. His name was Paul and he was one of those men who had the knack of making a woman feel instantly special. Guys like him know how to use everything they've got to seduce you and that's exactly what he did. He wasn't a high achiever. He was nice looking but not as handsome as Tony or as gorgeous as Ben. He was, however, a very sexual, sensual person and I was extremely attracted to him! I was getting absolutely nothing from Ben at the time so I lapped it all up.

Looking back, I wish I'd made a clean break with Ben. I was still in love with him and always hoped things would change back to what they once had been. Paul was actually on the scene for two months before we started seeing each other regularly. I liked him but knew in my heart that he wasn't right for me. He had a totally different lifestyle and outlook to mine, one that mostly involved going down the pub and drinking, which I really wasn't into. I guess he was my bit of rough. At one stage I thought I'd fallen in love with him but it was just unadulterated, pure lust. He was sexy, tactile, had the right moves and said the right things – what you'd call an excellent diversion.

Ben had been having affairs for years but I didn't know this when I came clean and told him about Paul. The motivation for telling someone you're cheating on them is an interesting one and I guess it can vary from needing to unload your guilt to hoping to galvanise them into action and making them realise what's at stake. My own desire to tell Ben probably arose out of the latter. When I told him he went ballistic. I felt very bad about it and we decided to split up for two weeks during which time he went off to Ibiza with his friends for a break. While I knew it would involve drugs, I didn't even consider it would involve other women. He returned from Ibiza the day before we were supposed to be going away to Hawaii for a holiday. Despite everything that was going on we had not changed our plans, but I was worried about him. He seemed unwell and again I had no idea it was because of his drug use. I ended up calling the doctor who examined him and probably knew drugs were involved. He told Ben to make sure he drank lots of fluids. After the doctor left Ben confessed he had been taking five 'E's a night.

The next day we set off for the airport to catch our BA flight to Hawaii. Ben began to get very restless and just couldn't settle in his seat. At one point he got up to go to the toilet but he didn't get there. Much to my horror he was talking and gesticulating to the stewardesses in a state of what I started to realise was now serious agitation. In fact, he was having a panic attack. I immediately knew the drugs were still working on him. By this time the stewardesses were starting to get anxious. They asked him nicely if he would go and sit down. His reply was that he couldn't because he was going to have a heart attack and they would have to stage an emergency landing. I approached them and asked them to let me calm him down. They were not too pleased but eventually I persuaded them. I took him into the toilet, talked to him calmly and gave him water until I could see he was starting to settle. Eventually he calmed right down and the rest of the flight continued uneventfully. It was one of the scariest episodes I have been through. The inside of a plane is no place to be coming off a major drug trip.

Hawaii was beautiful but I don't think we enjoyed it as much as we should have since Ben chose the holiday to confess he'd been having an affair. He assured me they had only met a couple of times and he blamed it on me neglecting him because I was too preoccupied with my work. I really think that is one of the weakest excuses you can make since it could apply to most people! It's just too convenient. I was devastated because I felt it was partly his behaviour that had driven me to the affair with Paul. I wasn't proud of what I'd done; in fact, I was really upset that I'd had an affair. I just wanted us to be how we used to be. We argued constantly and in the end I came home early, leaving him there on his own.

Unfortunately, the airplane experience made little difference to Ben and he wasn't going to stop taking drugs – definitely not in the near future anyway. Our relationship was pretty well doomed from that point on. I still didn't know about the other women in his life but there was at least one other occasion when I had strong suspicions about an affair. He managed to convince me nothing was going on. Consequently I began increasingly to blame myself for much of what had gone wrong with our relationship. I took responsibility for our problems because I was the one having an affair. Instead of being angry about the effect that drugs were having on him and subsequently our relationship, I looked upon his drug taking as something I should be helping him with.

We had decided it would be better if Ben moved into his own place, which he did in November 1994. When we weren't busy splitting up I would go round there. I thought it was very odd that when I came over the phone was always off the hook. When I questioned him about it he said it was because his drug dealer kept pestering him. He obviously thought I was stupid enough to swallow anything but this time I wasn't convinced; I knew something was up. One night when I was there with him he'd forgotten to unhook the phone and it started ringing. He refused to answer it, again saying it was the drug dealer annoying him. He then made the crucial mistake of getting into the shower. I dialled 1471 and got the number. Then, in a move which would make any private detective proud, I waited for his phone bills to arrive. All I had to do was check his front porch when he was out, which was quite often. When his Vodaphone bill arrived I methodically went through the numbers and there was one that seemed to come up about the same time as he was doing shows. I didn't stop there: I scanned his credit card bill and found he'd been to Interflora. I went to the florist but they wouldn't tell me who received the flowers so I offered them a goody bag of Ann Summers products, which made them very helpful. The card for the flowers had been written to a woman called Kate. It said, 'Sorry for last night, hope you're feeling better. Lots of love. Ben.' The flowers had been sent to a Lloyds Bank in Leeds.

I knew Ben had just done a show at a hotel in Leeds so I decided to challenge him. He went into a wild temper, ranting both at me and the florist. He was furious and immediately went on the attack. His story was that one of his friends had been having an affair with this girl and Ben had felt sorry for her one night when his friend hadn't been nice to her. So he thought it would be a good idea if he sent her some flowers. Now, I may have led a sheltered life but, honestly, did he think I was going to buy that? He evidently didn't because when I rang Kate he had obviously primed her. She told me exactly the same story. I later found out that the real reason he'd sent her the flowers was because of something that happened when they'd all been taking a drug called GHB, also known as the 'date rape' drug. Three of them – Ben, Kate and one of Ben's friends – had then passed out on the bed. During the night the other guy had sex with Kate, without her knowledge. In the morning she realised what had happened and was naturally very distressed.

I didn't learn the full extent of Ben's various infidelities until after we'd split up for good in April 1998. I'd carried a lot of guilt because I thought I hadn't put enough effort into the relationship. I have since wondered if that was a little of my mother coming out in me. Although I hated the fact that she spent so much time trying to please John and feeling bad when he wasn't happy, here I was doing exactly the same. I know Ben had treated me badly but I was also wrong in having the affair with Paul. In the end I told Ben I wanted a break. Meanwhile I decided to make a proper go of it with Paul. It all became very messy when Ben caught us together and insisted that I had not said I wanted a break when I took up with Paul! I ended up splitting up from them both, which was probably the best thing that could have happened.

My view is that we both contributed to the breakdown of our relationship. I wish I could have accepted it wasn't going anywhere earlier but hindsight is a wonderful thing. In many ways we were so compatible but unfortunately Ben's drug taking overtook the relationship and became the central focus of our life, so we really didn't have a chance. Somewhere in the middle of it all was the real Ben, the funny, stimulating, charming man I had fallen for. After I left him I think he made a big effort to settle down. He's doing well as a salesman, has a lovely wife and they have a baby. Due to health problems, he's also stopped doing drugs.

CHAPTER SIX

Too close for comfort

The latter years with Ben were dramatic enough but, as we know, life likes to deal challenges out in job lots. In 1997 I found myself being held to ransom by two people who thought they could coerce me into doing what they wanted. Since becoming successful and having a public profile, I've increasingly encountered people who take the attitude of, 'I'm poor, you're rich, therefore you can afford to pay.' Some of these have been friends (not any more). Despite what people may think about my dad's influence, my achievements are not the result of being born with a silver spoon in my mouth and I would not want it that way. I admire my dad immensely and his support and advice have been invaluable, but I have had to prove myself. Even so, I had to put up with a lot of scepticism – and sexism – to get to where I am, probably more than a lot of people, and I still encounter resistance from some quarters. I've paid my dues and the idea that opportunists can just come along and try to take advantage really angers me.

One of these was Dominic O'Shea, the photographer who'd worked for us at Ann Summers and who'd taken the sexy pictures of Vanessa and me four years earlier. We hadn't heard of him since he disappeared after his accident in 1993, and when he returned the rumour was that he was broke. In February 1997 I received a letter from him. It said that he wanted £2 million for all the photographs he'd taken for our catalogues over the years. The modus operandi of catalogue shoots is usually this: when we do a shoot, the photographer takes the photographs, gives them to us and we pay an agreed fee. The photographer owns the copyright but it's largely irrelevant since we don't use the photos for anything else – they're just stuck in the archives and left to gather dust. Then, six months later, we do a totally fresh shoot and the same process takes place. Photographers will not usually demand the photos back.

Dominic, however, had something else on his mind, namely *money*. His premise was that if he didn't get all the photographs back he would sell the intimate pictures of Vanessa and me. I had no choice but to bring in lawyers, which was somewhat embarrassing since they insisted on being shown the pictures Dominic had taken of us. They seemed to scrutinise them a bit too slowly. That was probably one of the most uncomfortable meetings I've ever had in my life! The whole episode was especially distressing because the photos had been taken by someone who was, at the time, a friend. In the end, I called his bluff and asked my staff to search the archives for every catalogue picture he'd ever done. We sent him everything we had along with a confidentiality agreement and £2,000 for the rights. It worked.

I don't know what was in the air in early 1997, but about the same time as Dominic resurfaced I received a very odd letter at my home address in Caterham. It was written in a childish hand and was signed by someone called 'Jason'. Jason wrote that he had a brother 'who was out of control', who was going to hurt me. It stated that if I wanted to know more then I should go to the Rose and Crown pub which was right next door to my offices in Surrey, where I would receive a telephone call on the pub's phone at a certain time.

I was scared and, in retrospect, should perhaps have alerted the police at that point. But I was also curious because I couldn't work out how someone had obtained my home address and my postcode. I wanted to take the phone call. I called my sister, told her what had happened and read her the letter. I told her I'd decided I would be in the pub to take the call and asked her to come with me. At the back of my mind I also had the thought that it might be something to do with Ben. At that point our relationship was on its last legs and, don't ask me why, but I thought maybe it was the boyfriend of the girl in Leeds who'd cooked up some sort of silly scheme. I had never set foot in the Rose and Crown, but that day, a Saturday, I went there in good time to receive the call. Suddenly the girl behind the bar called my name.

The caller sounded like he was about sixteen and had an air of innocence about him. The pub was naturally very noisy so I couldn't hear him properly and had trouble making out what he was saying. At the same time the girl behind the bar was getting impatient and told me I had to come off the phone. I did something I probably would not do again: I gave him my mobile so he could ring me. I'll admit I was curious but rationalised that I could always change the number. He told me he would call back in an hour so I went home and, sure enough, the phone rang. He explained that his older brother was a thug and had said he wanted to harm me. I still didn't believe him. We talked for quite a while and he told me his brother had been paid to do a job on me. His reason for contacting me was that while he was terrified of his brother, he himself knew the difference between wrong and right. I felt a bit sick in the stomach listening to this but I wanted to keep him talking so I could find out exactly what he knew about me. He was in a call box somewhere and having to put quite a lot of money in the coin machine. He denied that he knew anything about me but as he spoke he let slip a couple of details that suggested he knew the house. He also knew that I had security cameras.

At that stage I was more convinced that this was a young boy with a crush who wanted to gain my attention. I said, 'Look, I think you have a crush on me. I don't want you to contact me again.' I hung up on him. The next day while I was shopping in M&S in Croydon he rang me again. In fact, he rang me thirty times in one hour! I switched off the phone and decided to ignore him. I really felt this guy was a teenage crank.

On Monday morning, however, all that changed. I received a call on the office phone from a woman claiming to be Jason's mother. She said that everything he was saying was true. She sounded older – she was sixty-four, as it turned out – and said Jason was upset about the whole thing. He suffered from asthma and was having really bad attacks because he was worried about me. It was at that moment I realised it wasn't just a teenager with a crush but something much more sinister. The woman begged me to talk to Jason again. I said I would, and when he called he told me that his brother was planning to ram my car at the traffic lights. 'It won't be at your house because you've got CCTV there,' he said. He also said he knew that my boyfriend at the time was doing drugs. He told me he lived in Caterham, near the local chippie. He then suggested that we meet in a local churchyard. It was time to go to the police.

I went to Croydon police station. The detective constable did not take it very seriously, despite all my evidence. He did, however, take notes and pass it on to his superior. The next day I received a telephone call from Scotland Yard who said they were very worried and came down to see me. I have to say, they were absolutely amazing and very helpful. They named the case 'Operation Lemon'. They were taking no chances and set up more CCTV at my home and told me to change the car I was driving, so I hired a rental car. I was also told not to go out without anyone accompanying me. I felt stifled, like a prisoner. While I did change my car, I still went out on my own and I suppose my defiance comes from my childhood: I was determined not to be a victim in any sense of the word and that included letting somebody have a hold over me. I'd been through all that with John – I'd been through much worse with him – and this was not going to break me. Sure, I might have been scared but I was also angry. I used to sit in my house that I'd worked so hard for, thinking, 'This is supposed to be my sanctuary and I don't feel safe.' I used to wonder if it might even be a neighbour. As a child I'd known what it was like to be constantly tortured by the threat that something might happen to me. I'd lived all those nights in my bedroom as a young teenager, hoping and praying that John would not choose to come in and sexually abuse me. Even when he was not around it was constantly playing on my mind. And now I had the thought that someone was out there, just waiting for their chance to come and terrorise me.

Jason cancelled our meeting in the churchyard at the last minute. The police had planned to catch him there but now they had another plan. They placed a recording device on my office phone so that they could record him, and so I had to persuade him to ring the office number. They were very kind and assured me that I would not have to be on the phone for more than just a couple of minutes for them to find out exactly where he was. The Detective Superintendent in charge, Steve Gwillam, gave me a lot of confidence. We set it up. My sister would be in another room listening. As soon as Jason called, Vanessa would ring Steve Gwillam so they could activate the trace from their end.

When the call came in on my mobile, I knew I was on a mission. I was at home and had to persuade him to call me back on my office number. I was so afraid it would fail but I hoped I'd persuaded him. I asked him to give me time to get to the office so he could call me back on that number. I drove like a maniac to get there and when I did I reversed into a parked car (I sorted it out later), I was in such a panic. The call came into the office and after a minute they were having trouble tracing him.

I was actually on the phone for an hour calmly talking to him and asking him questions about his life to try and keep him talking. He told me his brother had cut people's ears off. At the same time I was making hand signals to Vanessa, asking her if the police had found anything. No, not yet. By now he was in full flow, describing his brother's criminal activities, and I believed him and it terrified me. Suddenly Vanessa came back into the room and signalled to me that the police had traced the call. I could finally come off the phone but I was shaking uncontrollably. I can't say I was relieved at that point, especially since Jason had said he wanted to meet me. I thought they would just arrest him then and there but they didn't. Apparently he was attached to another crime so the police wanted to keep him under surveillance for a while.

It turned out that the reason it took so long to trace him was that he actually lived in Lincoln. His name was Dean Bentley, he was twenty-one, and apparently he'd driven down to my house at least three times and slept outside in his car. He'd read about me and found my home address and postcode on the electoral register. He'd made up the drug thing about Ben, which was quite spooky. It turned out it was all his idea. He'd read about me in the *Sunday Mirror* and persuaded his mum to hire someone to attack me so that he could save me and be my knight in shining armour. He'd written the scripts for his mother so she could speak to me on the phone. His mum, Olwyn, had found a thug and offered him £400 to do the job. They had already set a date, in April. When he was finally arrested – in March – they found he had photos of me that showed exactly where the knife was going in and how he was going to save me. But that's not all. After he'd saved me he would bring me flowers the next day. We would go to Skegness and live happily ever after. The police described him as a fantasist but to me the whole experience was terrifyingly real. He had terrorised me and invaded my life for three months and now I hoped I would get some justice.

I didn't attend the court. I went away to Portugal and watched the outcome of the trial on *Sky News*. Even with that distance between us, I found it very chilling and stressful; once Dean had been caught it seemed like everything I was keeping inside came to the surface. First I got tinnitus and then dermatitis – both stress reactions. To make matters worse, he was not given a custodial sentence. Nothing is simple where the legal system is concerned. Dean Bentley was put on probation for two years and ordered to do a hundred hours' community service, while his mother was given a conditional discharge. I was absolutely outraged. How could it be possible for two people who'd conspired to put me through hell to be let off so lightly? The answer was that they'd been charged under something called the Malicious Communications Act, which did not have provision for a custodial sentence.

I was to find out again just how hard it is to convict a stalker when, in 2005, a letter addressed to me was received at our offices. It was opened by my PA at the time, Sarah. Inside was a black and white photograph of a man who described himself as '56, 5 feet 11 inches, reasonably slim, with size 11 feet, and a frustrated polymath'. The letter was very garbled and didn't make a lot of sense, apart from the sexual references. It mentioned Vanessa a couple of times as well. The man wanted me to make contact with him and threatened it would be a 'massive mistake' if I didn't.

The next day this man went into our Brewer Street store and handed over a package for me to the Store Manager. The parcel was forwarded to my office. This time my Managing Director Julie Harris opened it and when she saw what was in it, she alerted security. Inside were some abstract oil paintings with a note attached, and a further letter. Again, the content was incoherent but referred to porn magazines, sex acts, my sister Vanessa and his 'luscious slut of an adopted daughter'. He also said that he had written to other high-profile females, talked about getting money from them and requested financial assistance from me.

Julie can sometimes be overly protective of me and, because I'd been having a tough time, she decided that I should have my holiday free of worry and that she would deal with the situation on my behalf. She called the police and met with two detectives to assess the risk to me. After the police made enquiries they reported back to Julie, saying that the letters were from a schizophrenic under medical treatment and they assessed him to be a serious threat. The police wanted to make me aware of the situation; however, Julie was insistent that I should have my break. The police went to the man's home several times that week to try to take him in for questioning, and hopefully have him restrained under the Mental Health Act. But he was never there.

On Monday morning, the day after I returned home, the detectives and Julie came over to explain what had been happening. What annoyed me was how unhelpful and even elusive the police were when we asked them questions about the man's previous convictions and what they thought the actual threat was. It was time to increase the security around my house, which we did. I also gave all the people who work for me at my house pictures of him so they'd know who to watch out for. The police told us they would continue to visit his property until they could arrest him. Three days later, on 7 July 2005, the bombings in London took place and the detectives involved in my case were moved over to Scotland Yard.

I didn't receive any further communication for a few weeks, although Julie insisted that she had seen him one day at the petrol station across the road from the office. The police were alerted, but they did not arrive in time to see the man. Then, on 16 August, what was to be the last letter from him arrived. It was not as explicit as the early ones he'd sent and the handwriting was better. Apparently the erratic writing and incoherent expression we'd seen previously indicated that he was not taking his medication. Nothing more was received from him and he was never charged with harassing me.

At the time I wondered what it would take for police to detain someone like him. What does it take for people like him to be considered dangerous? Unfortunately, often it's not until something tragic happens that these cases are taken as seriously as they should be. As I sit here over a year and half later, I see a report in the *Observer* newspaper that chills me: apparently one person in Britain a week is killed by a psychiatric patient who has been assessed as being low risk.

CHAPTER SEVEN

Concrete shoes and the nearest river

Everybody that knew Paul seemed quite surprised at the way he was smitten with me and they were equally amazed when his roving eye was put on hold after we first got together. After I'd split up from Ben I started to think that maybe the relationship with Paul could really work. Sure, he wasn't the most successful guy but I managed to encourage him to do something different, with more opportunity, and he started a job selling systems for an alarm company. He still wasn't the sort of man I'd normally go for but he was very sexy, charming and outgoing. Still, it's amazing what we women will convince ourselves of when we're feeling vulnerable. It's as if all that intelligence and rationality that carries us through the rest of life deserts us when we most need it!

We'd only been back together for a few months when I felt things weren't right. I was beginning to see the real Paul: the Jack the Lad character that everyone had warned me about. I should have realised this relationship wasn't going anywhere and cut my losses. The fact that he moved his clothes in but not anything else suggested impermanence. On top of that, he was starting to change and was becoming less affectionate and loving.

By now I'd wised up to the possibility that my partner could be cheating, and I strongly suspected Paul was having an affair. My experience told me the signs were all there – the indifference, the lack of attention – but I needed proof. Being someone who doesn't do things by halves, and mindful of my previous experience, I decided to employ a private detective to get to find out the truth. The trouble was that Paul was whizzing around the South East in his car for work and the private detective couldn't keep up with him. However, he did manage to find out that Paul was popping into a particular sports shop in Sutton every now and then. There was a girl working there and he thought that she was probably the one that Paul was seeing.

The detective decided to follow the girl from the shop, because it was easier than keeping up with Paul's driving and would hopefully produce the same result. He managed to put a transmitter in her bag and followed her home. A few days before that Paul had lost his keys. As I was helping him look for them I'd found a receipt for two sun loungers. I remember saying, 'What's this for?' Paul's response was that he collected them so he could put them through for tax reasons. I didn't think anything of it until the detective rang to say he'd been outside the girl's house, watching, for three hours. Paul had eventually turned up and taken two sun loungers from the boot of his car. I later found out they were her birthday present. Paul then went in and the detective saw the upstairs curtains close. This confirmed what I suspected: Paul *was* having an affair.

To put it bluntly, I was gutted. The detective then gave me the girl's phone number and I decided to put into action the plan I'd hatched. I left the office and Vanessa came back with me to my house. With her help, I packed up Paul's clothes in bin liners and put them by the front door. The idea was to entice him back home as quickly as possible. The best way I could think of was to tell him one of my friends had called in while I was working from home and wanted an alarm system for her house. I rang Paul and told him he had to come home now since this was the only time she could make it. Never one to miss a sale, he said he was on his way.

It wasn't long before he pulled up in the drive. Seeing the bin bags, he said, 'What's all this about?' I told him I was kicking him out. He asked why and I replied that I knew he was having affair. I wasn't going to tell him how I found out. He kept asking who told me. I just told him to go. What happened next did not figure in my scenario. For some reason he grabbed my car keys, bundled the sacks of his clothes into the boot of my car and drove off. 'Oh my God,' I thought, 'he's stolen my car.' I was outraged but there was nothing I could do except call the police. First, though, I rang Vodaphone and told them my boyfriend's phone had been stolen and could they please disconnect it? They were very obliging and said they would do so immediately. I didn't want him to contact the girl he was seeing before I could get to her. I'd been here before.

I'm not the sort of woman who loses her temper easily and I was in a relatively calm frame of mind as I dialled the number. 'Hello,' I said, 'I'm Jacqueline Gold.' 'I know of you,' she said, as if she was expecting me. I continued. 'I believe my boyfriend is having an affair with you.' But hearing me say that, she was absolutely shocked. 'Oh, my God. We're engaged to be married and I'm three months pregnant,' she replied. 'He told me he was living in a bedsit.' At this point we were obviously both quite distraught at having discovered Paul's double deception but neither of us seemed to know what to say next. 'And by the way,' I said coolly, 'he's stolen my car.'

I came off the phone and then rang the police. They didn't seem very interested at first, and I'm positive that if it hadn't been for the policewoman feeling sorry for me, they wouldn't have bothered with the case. Paul had gone back to the girl and kept my car. The police kept ringing me with promises that they'd help me but nothing happened. I imagine they thought of it as just another domestic issue and so I'd probably just dropped to the bottom of the list. Things had now dragged on for almost a month and I despaired of getting my car back. One day the helpful policewoman went with a colleague round to tell Paul to give it back to me and he was so abusive, they arrested him. He was handcuffed and taken to Reigate police station, which was miles away from where he lived, and I finally got my car back.

I don't go into relationships lightly, but once involved, I give 100 per cent. Then it goes wrong and I get very upset. It's not as if I thought Paul was Mr Right – he certainly wasn't – but sometimes you just can't help yourself and I did love him – or thought I did at the time. After we split up I started to get pains in my stomach. My periods were seriously heavy as well and I felt very strange so I went to see the doctor. I found out I'd had a miscarriage a week after Paul had left. I was very distraught. I'm a great believer in the effects of stress on our physical health and I've little doubt that finding out about the affair contributed to the miscarriage.

At least one good thing came from our relationship and that was meeting one of my best friends, Sandie, who was a friend of Paul's. Though I'd first met Sandie when Paul and I were still together, it wasn't until after I'd broken up with him that she and I really got to know each other. Sandie is sharp-witted, very funny and charismatic. She is also challenging, something I find very attractive in people. You just know that Sandie won't automatically agree with you. And if she disagrees she'll make a very strong case. On top of that I think she brings out my mischievous streak. In fact, I know she does!

Until I met Ben I didn't really have many girlfriends. Having had my social life restricted by my childhood, the idea of developing friendships wasn't a natural part of my life. When I met Tony he was quite protective and didn't want me to go out without him. That suited me fine at the time: I was in a new situation with a man I loved, so it presented no problems. Up until this point I'd had only brief friendships that drifted apart, such as with the girls at school, and then with the girls from Ben's gregarious social scene, where we were thrown together not really through choice.

One of the things I decided to do after Ben and I split up was to turn my birthday into a big occasion. I started having themed birthday parties, which involved a great deal of effort on my part, but it was an effort I enjoyed making. I've had an Andy Warhol Party, a White Party and a Tequila Party among others, and each has been more spectacular than the last. They have also meant that, as well as inviting people I know, I have met many new people, some of whom have become very dear friends. Carole is one of these.

I met Carole through Anna-Marie, a girl who had modelled for Ann Summers and who ended up marrying the footballer, Lee Hughes. Anna-Marie brought Carole along to my first themed party in 1998. My first impression of her was that she was very friendly, but a bit 'full on'. I think this was a reflection of the stage I was at. I didn't have any of what I would call real friends and I wasn't used to people being in my space. At one point she came up to me and said, 'I've heard you have written a book (my first book, *Good Vibrations*). I'm writing a book called *Me and My Shadow*.' Carole's book was about MS, an awful disease which she's managed to deal with very well. She is truly one of the sunniest characters I've ever met. After our initial meeting we met again and got on very well and I soon realised I had completely misunderstood her. Carole is exceptionally warm and friendly. I'd say she was my first true friend, my spiritual friend, a woman who brings light into my life whenever I see her. She carries a lot of positivity with her and puts me into a wonderful mood. Along with Sandie, she has since become part of a close group who I know will be my friends for life.

After splitting up with Paul I wasn't dating anybody, though I was spending a lot of time with a friend, Dave. Dave was part of Ben's crowd and I'd known him for several years. Ben was still ringing me and we were talking. 'You shouldn't be spending time with Dave,' he said. 'You can't trust him.' Thinking he was just jealous, I didn't take any notice. I should have, though. Dave was one of the leftovers from the Ben era and that should have been a warning in itself.

Dave and I got on well; we flirted but nothing more. I was happy to have a friend and not anxious to be involved with anybody. After two lengthy relationships, there was no doubt I needed some 'me' time to reflect, if nothing else. Christmas was approaching and the plan was that my sister Vanessa, her boyfriend Steve and Dave would spend Christmas with me at my house. Dave's young son would join us on the day. The house I was living in at the time, in Caterham, had three bedrooms. I would have mine, Vanessa and Steve would be in another, and Dave would be in the single room. It was Christmas Eve and we went off to Croydon to a bar called McCluskey's. We were all in good spirits and had a really great time, drinking and dancing. Vanessa and Steve left early and went home, while Dave and I partied on until closing time. Dave was quite drunk and he was telling anyone who would listen that he and I were going to get together that Christmas. We were definitely not together in the physical sense and I didn't think too much of what he was saying: I just took it as part of the whole Christmassy mood. Of course, I was flattered but I had no intention of getting involved with Dave. When we arrived home Vanessa and Steve were still up. I went and joined them in the lounge, and we were just sitting around talking when I began to feel completely overwhelmed by this strange tiredness. It was unlike anything I'd ever felt before and my head felt very weird. I decided that my night had to end there and wished everyone goodnight. I didn't understand what was going on since I had never experienced a feeling like this from alcohol. It was now about 3am.

Normally when I go to bed I leave the door open but on this night I closed it just to let Dave know there was no invitation. I got myself ready for a long night's sleep: it was a very cold night so I wore a nightshirt and socks to keep warm and as soon as I got into bed I was out for the count. It felt like I hadn't been asleep long when I woke up and everything looked blurred. I wasn't sure what I was seeing but I could just make out a face in front of me. I couldn't actually tell where it was. It was out of register, a bit like seeing something in pixels. I then discovered I couldn't move my body; it was as if I was paralysed. I could just about turn my head slightly, and out of the corner of my eye could see that the time on the clock was 5am. Then I realised that Dave was in bed next to me and I remember saying, 'What are you doing?' He said, 'Oh, don't be like that.' I was angry but I could barely raise the energy to say, 'What are you doing in my bed?' I wanted to leap out but I couldn't move. 'I just think we'd be so good together,' he said. 'Vanessa knows I'm in here and she thinks we'd make a great couple.'

By now I could feel myself drifting in and out of consciousness. I can categorically state that I had never felt anything like this ever before – or since. I suspect that he may have given me a 'date-rape' drug, which was not unknown in his circle of friends. I remember telling him to get out of my bed and then drifting off again. When I came to, there was Dave, wanking right next to me. I'd known this man for ten years and thought we had a strong friendship. Thank God he didn't rape me. He finished himself off, then got up and went to the bathroom. When he returned, he kissed me on the forehead and said, 'I'm really sorry,' and then went back to his room. I still couldn't move anything except my head and my vision was severely impaired. I then drifted back into semi-consciousness.

Christmas Day felt very surreal. I was sitting alone in the kitchen in my dressing gown, trying to make preparations for Christmas dinner, with this sense of anger and indignation surging through me. I was furious and upset at Dave for betraying my trust. I was also wondering about the idea that my sister had encouraged him, which I doubted, but it was still bothering me. The incident brought back painful memories of the sexual abuse I'd suffered as a child and, like many others who've been in that situation, I began to question my own behaviour yet again. 'Had I created the situation? Was it my fault? Had I done anything to encourage Dave to come into my bedroom?' I reminded myself that I'd shut the door and made it clear where he was sleeping. Sure, we flirted when we were out but that's what lots of people do at Christmas. And I was quite sure I had been under the influence of something that was definitely not just alcohol, something I had not chosen to take. Otherwise, why did I lie there unable to move? It was all very confusing and, on top of that, there was the thought that I was just about to spoil everyone's Christmas. I adore the whole festive season and nothing is ever too much trouble. Over the years I've gone to great lengths to make Christmas as much of an occasion as possible, so the possibility that it was about to turn sour added to my distress.

Vanessa was the first person downstairs. She has since told me that I looked like a woman possessed. 'I cannot believe you encouraged him last night,' I said angrily. She looked completely blank so, feeling myself shaking, I told her what happened. She was absolutely horrified and said she'd never done anything of the sort. Our Christmas plans were in disarray and I told Dave in no uncertain terms he had to leave. (He needed to stay at the house until his young son was dropped off, as there was no alternative way for them to meet up by that point.) I don't know whether it was a nervous reaction or what, but Vanessa's boyfriend, who was a friend of Dave's (and Ben's), just stood there, laughing. I couldn't believe it.

We were all supposed to be flying in one of my father's company's Gold Air planes to Madrid for New Year's Eve to see Cirque du Soleil. Between Christmas and New Year Dave bombarded me with phone calls and messages, saying he regretted what he had done and was very sorry. I didn't pick up the answer machine, having decided that I would deal with him when I was ready, which I did. I phoned him just before New Year's Eve and told him what I thought and that there was absolutely no question of us ever being friends again, which meant he wasn't coming to Madrid and I never wanted to see him again. Vanessa got rid of her boyfriend not long after that. We were both in with a bad crowd but neither of us realised it. They covered it well. But they were gone now. In my head Dave had metaphorically gone to a place where I dismiss people who've done the wrong thing by me, simply by saying 'concrete shoes and the nearest river'. It just means they will never be allowed back in my life again.

Irish eyes not smiling

O'Connell Street is Dublin's main thoroughfare, a major shopping precinct and also one of the widest streets in Europe. Halfway along the street is the imposing GPO building, once the headquarters of the Irish provisional government. It's also been the scene of some bitter conflicts between the Irish and the British and you can still see bullet holes in the columns of the building. In 1999 I was to face my own battle over a piece of O'Connell Street when we decided to open a shop there. I didn't know it at the time but it would test all my courage and resolve.

While run to a formula, our party plan operation is open to regional differences, both in the way it is received and the revenue it brings in. We've found, for example, that the further north you go, the less inhibited people are. Without wanting to offend southerners, it seems northerners are more relaxed and sociable and the parties there are always much more raucous. Then there is Ireland, which is easily one of our most profitable markets. In fact, our party plan operation there is much more profitable than in the UK. Following the success of party plan, we had decided to expand our retail operation, a project we embarked on in 1995. Between then and 2001 we opened fifty-two stores. Since party plan had done so well for us in Dublin, it seemed only logical that this wonderful city should be part of our retail expansion programme.

We found a fantastic location on O'Connell Street which was larger than any store premises we had at the time. Our research indicated that if we opened there we would do very well. Things seemed to be progressing well until, in July 1999, I received a letter from one of the councillors from the Dublin Corporation. Its premise was pretty clear: he was asking me not to open. He felt – *they* felt – that a store like Ann Summers would be totally inappropriate for O'Connell Street and for Dublin.

I wasn't pleased but I know I'm a good communicator, especially on the subject of my business, and decided that I would be able to change their preconceived ideas about our stores. I wrote back to them and invited them to come over and meet us. The idea was that they would see the organisation for the corporate business it was, which would hopefully neutralise their image of us as some hidden, shady operation. I'd spent a lot of my career changing people's perceptions and felt strongly that I would be able to do so this time. The Project Manager, Ciaran McNamara, flew over with a colleague called Allan Taylor, who was the chief valuer for the Dublin Corporation. I had planned things meticulously, arranging for John Clarke, my Retail Director at the time, and Vanessa, who was not only Buying Director but also adept at liaising with local councils in the UK, to give them a tour of a couple of our stores. After that they would be shown around our head office and then we would sit down for a meeting. At this time we were still based in our original building, Gadoline House. It was prominently located on the main A22 but looked deceptively small from the outside. Much of the warehouse was on the lower ground floor, and both offices and warehousing stretched far back beyond what the eye could see, behind the BP garage next door.

Most of the offices were located at the front of the building on three levels. The warehouse was massive, with further offices running along each side. The main boardroom was at the front of the building on the top level. There was a large boardroom table, which was big enough to accommodate large area sales meetings, and the room had an ambience to impress both the bank manager and potential franchisees.

We were all sitting there in the boardroom and right from the start the atmosphere was very tense. As a businesswoman I am not unused to dealing with difficult situations and have certainly proved myself to be a successful negotiator; however, sometimes you just know that even if you were the world's most experienced diplomat you would not be able to find a way through. I immediately realised that what I had sitting before me were two men who were determined to be difficult. I was at the head of the table. Vanessa was on my immediate left with Allan Taylor sitting next to her, who, as far as I could tell, didn't look me in the eyes throughout the whole meeting. In fact, it seemed to me he didn't want to look at me at all! Perhaps he thought I was some sort of scarlet woman, who knows?

Ciaran was sitting next to me, with John Clarke on his right. He obviously found the meeting equally difficult. During the conversation he proclaimed, 'I don't have a problem with Ann Summers. I love sex.' I said I wasn't interested in his personal views about sex, but I was very interested in our store and the progression of our business. I had been trying to explain very carefully who our target audience were, how they were normal people who were a far cry from the dirty raincoat brigade. They were people who'd often been together for a while and who wanted to add some harmless fun to their sex lives. I had facts and figures, but Ciaran was not listening to my argument. He seemed intent only on relaying his pre-prepared views which bore no relation to what I had been saying. I'd had enough. Having invited them over for what I thought would be a civilised discussion, I was not even being heard.

'Look,' I said, 'let's just stop for a minute. You're not interested at all in what I have to say, are you?' Ciaran's response took me aback. 'There are a lot of nasty people in Ireland and I can't be held responsible for what might happen to you if you go ahead and open this store.' What was he trying to say? What sort of advice was he trying to give me? 'Oh my God,' I thought, 'He's concerned about the IRA.'

I managed to compose myself and then said, 'Look, you haven't come to consider my side of the story or negotiate, have you?' Ciaran admitted I was right. So I did the only thing you can do in those circumstances: I brought the meeting to an end.

I am not a woman who scares easily and the meeting just made me more determined to carry on. That's exactly what we did. We didn't panic; we just carried on making plans for the store.

Ciaran's concern that there were some nasty people out there turned out to be well founded. One day we received an anonymous letter through the post, addressed to me at one of our London stores. It contained a bullet, a real bullet. There was a note with it:

THERE ARE PLENTY OF FREELANCE PROVOS WHO WOULD DO A NICE ARSON JOB ON YOUR CESSPIT SHOP FOR A FEW HUNDRED QUID IF YOU DARE SET UP ON OUR MAIN STREET. YOU'LL NEED VERY HEAVY SECURITY. JUST STAY AWAY. YOU WHORE!!

Colleagues and friends were very worried, with some begging me not to go ahead. Initially, I was terrified but I also wasn't going to be bullied.

I was to go over a few days before the store opening in October 1999. I had security to meet me at the airport because I had no idea who or what I was dealing with. I'd also hired a Dublin-based publicity team. I wasn't totally happy with doing this, preferring to use my own London team, but I thought that, given the situation, it might be a good idea to go with locals who had the knowledge. I had also received a phone call earlier that week from the producers of *The Late Late Show*. I learnt that this was a popular TV talk show that reached a lot of people and they wanted me to appear. At the time my media experience was still very limited. Although I wanted publicity for the store I decided that since there had been such a furore about it already – the councillors from the Dublin Corporation were continuing to make waves in the newspapers – it would be best not to do the show.

I arrived in Dublin and went to meet with the publicity team. We discussed *The Late Late Show* and they insisted that I should appear, saying it would be the ideal opportunity for me to put my case forward in my own terms. Up till now Dublin had only heard the other side of the story. I was still very nervous about it but figured that if they thought it was a good idea, I should do it. Michael Crawford was on before me to launch his autobiography and was entertaining the live audience with his anecdotes – they seemed to be having a good time. 'I hope he's softened them up,' I thought. It was now my turn. The presenter Pat Kenny was sitting on the stage, behind a desk which obviously put him in a commanding position. I sat in a chair next to the desk. My heart was thumping by now and as I scanned the audience, I saw that Ciaran McNamara and Allan Taylor were straight ahead of me, right at the front. I had been set up!

From the start, the presenter took the tough approach with me. He wasn't exactly Jeremy Paxman but he seemed determined to get me into a corner. I was equally determined to make my point. I said, 'You know we have had Ann Summers parties in Dublin for years. We are successful because women love them just like they will love our store. Why should they be deprived because a man doesn't think it's right?' I pointed out that I heard no good, factual reason as to why the shop should not open. The presenter decided to involve the audience. Predictably, he threw the first question to Ciaran.

Ciaran stood up. He's a councillor so he's used to making his pitch in front of a public audience. I was thinking, 'Oh God, I'm going to die up here. I am going to be ripped apart.' When he'd finished the presenter pointed to one of the women in the audience and asked her what she thought. It was a brilliant moment. She just cut loose. 'Who does the Dublin Corporation think they are, telling women where we can and can't shop?' I had underestimated these Irish ladies. More of them joined her and they all turned on Ciaran. The debate continued to open up and widen. 'There's a newsagents that sells porn and you haven't closed that,' someone said. Somebody else thoughtfully pointed out that drug users were openly seen in the area and nothing had been done about them.

For me this was the icing on the cake. I had opened the store just before going to do the show. We'd been issued with a writ by the Dublin Corporation to close us down but I had decided I was going to take it all the way to court if I had to. We put together a petition on the day and got an overwhelming positive response. We had a record number of people through the doors on the day we opened and we haven't looked back: Dublin is now one of our top three best-performing stores. Eventually we did go to court and we won, with the result that the Dublin Corporation ended up paying our £20,000 costs.

The next day's papers echoed public opinion and went on the attack against the Dublin Corporation and their performance on the television programme. I, on the other hand, was commented on for my demeanour and also for the tasteful pale pink suit I wore. I obviously wasn't the sex slut in cheap red lace and skintight PVC that everyone had expected.

Later on I tried to arrange a meeting with the Irish Prime Minister. Not expecting him to oblige, I was very pleased to see that he at least sent his second in command, Jerry Hickey. I met him in the Dublin store and told him what we were trying to achieve. He was very supportive, a complete contrast to the Dublin Corporation.

Now we have five other stores in Ireland and they are all very well received. To illustrate how times have changed, when we opened in Cork the Mayor wanted to have his picture taken in the store. He knew the value of good publicity! The O'Connell Street store is now one of the highlights for visitors on the Dublin tour bus. I haven't heard the commentary but I would like to think they say something like, 'This is the scene of a major battle between Ann Summers and the Dublin Corporation. As you can see, the lady won.'

CHAPTER NINE

Minding my business

When I reflect on my move into Ann Summers I think I was very brave. I walked into a situation where I was totally inexperienced, I wasn't getting total support from the board and I had the handicap of being related to the owner so I had far more to lose. I was being driven only by gut feeling, by the responses from women I'd met at that first party I attended in Thamesmead and my own self-belief. It is not easy to step into an industry that is dominated by men and has an image that is more sleaze than sensuality. But that's what being an entrepreneur is all about. You have to take risks and go where others are too afraid to be. That's the thrill and it's also the difference between people who have ideas and those who make them happen: the latter step outside their comfort zone. And they don't stop once they've tasted success. Being an entrepreneur is not just about making money: if that is your only motivation your business will fail. You need to be hungry for success, to want to build something and put your own stamp on the world.

As the business developed, so did the challenges and the competition. Just after we started, a company called Silver Rose suddenly appeared on the scene. The man who ran it, Geoff Silver, had one shop selling erotic underwear and he wanted to set up a party plan scheme. What better way than to poach some of my people? Chris Rogers and Ann Galea decided to go off and join him. They took thirty of the women they'd recruited with them. This was literally only a year or so after we'd started which was bad news, not so much in terms of the people we lost but in trying to make sure that the remaining sales organisers were not discouraged, so one of my key tasks at this point was to ensure that morale remained high. Some of them took the defections to Silver Rose quite personally and, although I tried to point out to them that life goes on, they decided to leave as well. Nonetheless, our recruitment rate was very high, at about thirty new party organisers each day, so we recovered quickly.

Expansion is necessary for a business but it brings with it a lot of risks. In 1989 I employed a woman called Joyce Greenhill to run the party plan operation in the north. I had known for some time that we should be operating up there but it would have been foolish to try and run the process from our southern base. Joyce was very good at what she did and helped us get organised for our northern operation. In a way the party plan business organises itself: you train some people up, they recruit others and it perpetuates itself. As we progressed, I began to feel that Joyce wasn't quite right for us. Yes she could do the job, but there were things about the way in which she did it that weren't right. We now needed to project a more sophisticated image and I felt she was not going to be the right ambassador for our brand. The people I needed were a lot more polished and professional: that was the image I had been working hard to cultivate for myself and it was what I expected from my senior staff.

There are many people in business who are uncomfortable with change and I think Joyce was one of them. She didn't like the formalities of the business, formalities that become necessary whenever you grow in size, which was what was happening to Ann Summers. The more people you have, the more necessary it is to put in structures, otherwise you end up with chaos. I think Joyce felt we could just continue as we had always done, but becoming a bigger version of that. Not surprisingly, she was unhappy, so that when a company named Lovelace came calling, she was flattered. Lovelace was owned by a man called Carl Slack and we hadn't considered them major rivals. Fundamentally, Joyce wanted a directorship or she would leave. I said no and she went – and so did many of our party organisers. She was actively poaching them, forcing me to enact a campaign of damage limitation. I spoke to our organisers and told them to handle the defectors with good grace by letting those who were leaving know they were always welcome at Ann Summers. We lost around 500 ladies in all. Less than a year later Carl Slack's business was in trouble. I saw an opportunity to buy him out and get my staff back. It wasn't that easy. We bought the party plan channel of Lovelace but many of the ladies, fed up with the politics of the whole thing, decided that party plan was no longer for them. The deal meant we wouldn't lose any more staff and we gained a few back, but that was about it. The poaching issue was to rear its head again in 1994, when a company called Intrigue, in what was quite a brazen move, placed ads that said, 'Ann Summers girls wanted.' However, they continued trying to steal our party organisers. Intrigue had employed one of our ex-area managers and were effectively targeting our sales force with their ready-made lists of our people. In other words, they were setting up a company using stolen lists without doing any of the hard work or training or bearing any of the costs. We were actually preparing for full-scale legal battle when we heard they had gone into receivership. I will not hesitate in calling in top lawyers to fight anyone who tries to steal our business and I will go to any lengths to protect the business from anyone who dares to unlawfully or unethically jeopardise the Ann Summers brand.

As Ann Summers became more successful, I had more money to reinvest in the business and was planning for the future. By the early 1990s we were growing 20 per cent year on year. By 2001, having expanded the number of Ann Summers stores to fifty-two, we also had enough evidence to realise that our retail operation was not siphoning off business from party plan: in fact, it was helping increase party bookings. In the following four years we opened eighty-three more stores. We were very careful to ensure that the shops communicated to the customers in the same way as the party plan business. That meant they had to reflect the same brand image and the same ethos of being fun, female-friendly places that women wanted to visit. In February 2000 the high-street chain, Knickerbox, came up for sale. I was very interested and not just because I knew it would be relatively cheap. At this time Ann Summers was still struggling with credibility and I felt that not only was Knickerbox a good fit with our business, but it would add something positive to our brand. I had tried to buy it a few years earlier when it came up for sale, but failed. Now they were really in trouble it was time to get serious.

At the time Knickerbox was losing £5 million a year and I knew it was just a matter of time before they went into receivership. That might sound a bit vulture-like but it's the way business operates – why pay more for a company when you can get it at a knock-down price? Of course, operating in this way is a gamble because someone else could come along and whisk it away from under your nose. This is exactly what happened when I tried this tactic with

La Senza, which was snapped up by the owner of Rymans, Theo Paphitis. Theo is one of the dragons on the television programme, *Dragons' Den*. This time I was determined to do the deal. I went to meet the owner, the very brash and colourful Gary Klesch. He is one of those people who is in every sense larger than life and greeted me wearing a cowboy hat and cowboy boots. He must have stood at about 6 feet 5 inches. There was a pretty blonde at reception and, all in all, I felt like I'd stumbled into JR Ewing's office!

Klesch had set himself up as a 'distressed debt' specialist, rescuing companies in trouble but since he'd acquired Knickerbox he hadn't really done anything with it. I bought Knickerbox two weeks later and it was very cheap. I did a deal where I cherry-picked the best stores out of the fifty they had. We incorporated them into our existing infrastructure, which made it much more economical to run. I also put Knickerbox concessions into Ann Summers stores. This was a strategic move designed to introduce Knickerbox customers to Ann Summers, on their terms. These were people who would have liked to go into an Ann Summers store but still felt a little unsure of being in there. By putting a Knickerbox into the store, it meant they could go in and identify items with which they felt comfortable. Of course, they would then relax enough to do what they really wanted to do, which was look at the Ann Summers range. Because of this, footfall (the number of people coming into the shop) increased and our sales at Ann Summers increased by a considerable 15 per cent on top of the new sales generated from Knickerbox purchases.

With 145 stores and £145 million sales turnover, we're now mainstream; in effect we're a high-street brand. That means that we're exposed to the ups and down of the economic cycle, although not as much as other stores. One reason for this is that sex will always sell and even in a recessionary economy, sex toys and lingerie will still be doing brisk business as couples find themselves spending more time at home and decide they need to spice things up. We have consistently gone against retail trends and done well when the rest of the high street is struggling.

However, like other retailers, we are at the mercy of high rents and that can really impact on our bottom line. Fundamentally, the choice we have to make regarding sites is whether to be a destination store – a specialised and unique store where customers know our location and are willing to make a special visit. Destination stores will often be away from the main high street or shopping centre. The other alternative is to base ourselves in an 'A' location like a major shopping centre where you benefit from having loads of traffic already and are therefore in a position to capitalise on impulse buyers.

Quite often it is more profitable to be out of the way rather than in an expensive 'A' location. Once you offset your revenue against the rent it often works out better. In shopping centres such as Lakeside we are naturally affected by footfall, or lack of it, just like everyone else. It means that if people stay away from Lakeside then we lose out as well.

While most landlords welcome Ann Summers, there are some who still feel that we are not appropriate for their hallowed space. As I write, Bluewater are making it a bit difficult for us. The irony is that Bluewater did a survey and Ann Summers was the most requested store.

Party plan is very good for us and is even less susceptible to movements in the economy. During the miners' strike in 1984–85 party plan did very well. There were two reasons for this. One was that because men were out of work, women needed to supplement the family income, so they joined us as party organisers to earn a bit of extra money. The other reason we did well is that people were attending parties – having come with no intention of buying – and finding they only had to spend a little to return home with an item that would amuse them and their husbands!

I like to think that we have been responsible in some way for changing the attitudes of women – and men – towards sex. But you can't force products on to consumers if they don't want them in the first place. So our customers are also pushing their own boundaries. Women now are much more in the driver's seat with regard to exploring their

Mum and Dad when they first met, 1955

Left: Dad and me, aged five
Below: Mum and me, aged about six

Above left: Winning the school fancy-dress competition dressed as a squaw –
Mum always made me lovely costumes
Above right: Vanessa and me in our Maxi coats

Below left: Me about twelve, the time the abuse started
Below right: And at fifteen – towards the end

Me, aged seventeen,
with Martin

With Tony on
our wedding day,
2 August 1980

All dressed up for a conference with Janet Mudge, Party Plan Director (left), and Julie Harris, Managing Director (right)

THERE ARE PLENTY OF "FREELANCE" PROVOS WHO WOULD DO A NICE ARSON JOB ON YOUR CESSPIT SHOP FOR A FEW

HUNDRED QUID IF YOU DARE SET UP ON OUR MAIN STREET. YOU'LL NEED VERY HEAVY SECURITY. JUST STAY AWAY YOU WHORE !!

The anonymous letter I received with a bullet when setting up the Dublin store

Above: Dan, Nick, Vanessa and me – when everything was wonderful in 2002
Right: On the day of Vanessa's wedding, November 2002

Above: Vanessa, Dad and I, 2002
Left: My beloved Grandma
Rosie, aged 87
Below: Mum (left) and Auntie
Heather, 1998

The Times magazine, 16 November 2002 – me at work

My loyal team at Ann Summers headquarters

Vanessa, Sandie, Carole, Val, Joanna and me on our girlie
photo shoot, 2005

Dan and I, the night before we
broke up for good

Peaches, summer 2006

sexuality and I think that putting shops in the high street has helped this to happen. Instead of sex being seen as something hidden and taboo (unfortunately, that attitude does still persist) it is now seen as fun and something to enjoy, celebrate and explore. Our shops are warm, well lit and welcoming. Customers can browse the shop on their own but if they have any questions they will be answered by informed sales assistants who know their products and will make them feel comfortable. Despite our enviable sales figures we don't allow ourselves to become complacent. From the beginning I have always relied on my customers and staff for feedback, and listening to them has been a fundamental part of the success of the business.

There are still people, some of them women, who argue that the idea of women dressing up in sexy lingerie is not empowering at all because it is being done purely for men. The gist of their argument is that it is a step backwards. I find this faintly ridiculous since it presupposes that women do not enjoy feeling sexy and exploring their sexuality, and only do so for the pleasure of their men. It's a notion that completely ignores a woman's desire for pleasure and her ability to orchestrate it. As with many areas of their lives, this is about women taking the initiative, and that can only be a good thing.

At the same time it means that men are learning to understand that women can and will make their own decisions and demands with regard to sex. Years ago men weren't bothered whether women were enjoying themselves. Now men make an effort and want to please their partners and they like women to be confident – well, of course, there are still those that feel inadequate and struggle with the concept of a woman enjoying her sexuality but, in the main, men are more receptive, especially the younger generation, who understand that sex is not something you do to someone: it's something you do together. It's interesting to note that problems with attitude towards Ann Summers shops and products are often found among the older generation of men: I have come across difficult landlords of premises, or senior people in JobCentres where we have tried to recruit staff. I can only conclude that the existence of Ann Summers constitutes some kind of threat to them and makes them feel inferior or insecure.

Still, there are some places where you may not want to confront your sexuality. A few years ago Boots the chemists were considering adding sex toys to their shops. I like Boots but I wouldn't want to buy my sex toys from there. As I've often said to people, 'I buy my meat from the butchers, my shoes from a shoe shop and my sex toys from a shop that doesn't sell haemorrhoid cream.' At one point Tesco were also said to be thinking of it. Now I have nothing but admiration for Tesco; I think it is a brilliant brand. However, the thought conjured up this image of me pushing my trolley around the supermarket, loading it up with eggs, bacon, baguettes ... and a Rampant Rabbit.

Then I would get to the checkout, the bar code wouldn't work and there would be red faces all round. Are people ready for this? I don't think so.

CHAPTER TEN

Dad and I: a perfect team

It is frequently assumed that my father was very influential in getting me involved in the Gold Group. The truth is that it was my own choice and, until I decided to present my party plan idea back in 1982, I don't think he ever expected that I would become an integral part of the family business. Having produced two daughters but no sons, his expectation was that there would be nobody to succeed him. Now that person will be me. I accept it as a responsibility and see it as a natural extension of what I already do. It's a challenge I will take on with no difficulty since these are businesses I am involved in anyway and the same business philosophy and skills will apply. At the same time I don't want the day to come when he retires and I take over. Today he is Chairman of the Gold Group, I am its Chief Executive, and we are true business partners. At seventy he is extremely young for his age and very active, so hopefully we will continue working together for a long time to come.

*

The circumstances of my parents' divorce put a lot of distance between my father and myself and there is no question that our personal relationship started very late, probably about fifteen years ago. Despite his lack of direct influence over me when I was young, you can't discount the effects of genetics and I believe I take after him in so many ways. I love working with him and I especially enjoy the banter between us when we are discussing business issues. We went from having a very strained relationship, or very distant relationship, to becoming very close because all of a sudden we had something in common: passion for the business. In some ways that shared passion helped us get closer personally, and today he and I – and my sister – have more than made up for lost time. As well as business the three of us regularly share dinners, watch football and go on holiday.

Over the years his advice has been invaluable, not just because he is a clever man but also because I found there were limited networking opportunities open to me. One of the reasons for this is that Ann Summers was – and still is – regarded as a controversial business and other business-people just didn't want to be associated with us. At one point I joined the Direct Selling Association (DSA). Their conferences were very inspiring, with people from successful companies like Avon sharing their experiences. I once gave a speech there to a curious audience who were completely stunned when I told them what our turnover figures were. They had underestimated the professionalism and success of our operation. There were many questions afterwards. Did we really rely on customer feedback? Was our team made up of only women? Actually, the person who asked me the latter question was a man who ran a cosmetics business, Jaffra Cosmetics. It turned out he did not have one woman on his executive team, which I think is a huge mistake if you're in the beauty industry. His business went under not long after. In the end I felt the DSA was happy to have us as members, but, unlike their attitude towards other successful businesses, they continually failed to recognise our achievements. They refused to see that it didn't matter what product was being sold; I still had the same business and marketing issues as everyone else. They were more concerned about how their other members would react if we were recognised over others. When I said I was leaving the association, they pleaded with me to stay but I was already far too annoyed with the way I had been treated. Once my mind is made up, I rarely change it.

As a person my father is charming, articulate and a gentleman with a talent for storytelling. From his origins in the East End of London, he has taken the time to better himself, acquiring and enhancing his social skills. Dad is very much an opportunist. And as a businessman he knows his markets very well. Today the range of businesses owned by the Gold Group includes the *Sunday Sport* and Birmingham City Football Club, which he and Ralph own with David Sullivan. There is also a printing business, a property company with an expanding portfolio and shares in several other businesses. Until 2006, the Gold Group owned Gold Air International – the largest private jet company in the UK. We also had a publishing and distribution business involving several top-shelf magazine titles – I was quite influential in the sale of this business in 2006. Over the years the business of sex has changed in all sorts of ways: for one, the Internet has now overtaken the printed word. Maintaining a stable of top-shelf magazines in such a climate meant that resources were being used on a business which was no longer contributing as much to the Group as it once did.

My father's skill and passion is very much in logistics so at the beginning with Ann Summers he was heavily involved in stock control at the warehouse and would often be seen driving around on the forklift truck even on a Sunday afternoon, reorganising everything and improving systems. He has as high a regard for the work I am doing, as I do for him and, like any partners, we bring different things to the table. When I'm looking at the business I'm focused and won't let emotion stand in my way. I deal with issues very diplomatically and tactfully. However, my father prefers to sidestep any conflict involving disciplining or firing staff if he can. He doesn't like it at all and I find it quite endearing that this successful businessman, who has built an amazing business empire to become one of the UK's richest men, still worries about people's livelihoods. He finds it so difficult firing people that if he had his way we'd probably have five thousand employees instead of two thousand!

Sometimes you have no choice but to part company with people in business. People have to be right for the job and good enough to do it. At one time my father hired a man called Michael Vaughan. He was to be his right-hand man and would also help run the publishing side of the group, including our reprographic company, Z2. It soon became clear that his personality was not right for the culture of our businesses: he was too much like a Rottweiler and seemed to take delight in terrifying people, which would leave them demotivated. He definitely had designs on power and when Dad made him CEO of Gold Air International, he managed to go one step further and appoint himself as the Chairman! He also gradually began filling the company with his friends and family. He was someone who would always win an argument because he did it by browbeating everybody, a bit like some barristers do. He never let up and was so vocal that even the best businessmen forgot what their argument was. I took a different approach. Instead of trying to get a word in I would let him talk and talk. Meanwhile I would just listen and make detailed notes. He would eventually run out of steam at which point I would say, 'Now, Michael, I'd like to go over some of the points you made.' I knew he found my quietness unnerving. Every time I bumped into him he was quite edgy because he knew his bullyboy tactics didn't work with me and I would always challenge him where others wouldn't.

By August 2000 his attitude was out of control and there was no question in my mind that we had to get rid of him. I have to admit, however, there was something about him I liked. I didn't have to deal with this situation – it was nothing to do with me but it had got so bad that my father wouldn't deal with it and he refused any offers I made of doing it for him. In the end I knew the only way was to step in and fire him without telling Dad. The first step was to send him a letter – I think he knew it was coming – telling him I wanted to meet him at the Selsdon Park Hotel on a Friday afternoon. I'd already sat down with one of our lawyers and put together an exit package that included all the friends and family he'd hired, as well as himself. I had thought about it a lot and felt the package we'd worked out was very fair. Initially, I didn't tell my father what I was doing. I sent the letter off to Michael about a week before our meeting. Then, with about twenty-four hours to go until I was due to go to the hotel, I told my dad what was happening. Although I think Dad knew it had to be done, he just didn't like the whole messy business or the thought of all these people being out of a job.

Seeing how concerned my father was, I suggested he came over to see me while I was preparing for my meeting with Michael that afternoon. You have to handle situations like this with care and there was a great deal I had to think about. So there I am sitting in my study at home, working away, while my father is in the background, worrying about it and talking non-stop! I had never seen him like it before or since, but I understood he was dealing with somebody close to him and therefore there was a personal relationship involved. I briefed him on how I would deal with it and went off to the hotel. I was very calm. I'd also arranged for the solicitor who helped me put the exit package together to be in another room in the hotel so he could take over when I left. Michael arrived and the meeting went very smoothly. In situations like this I try to demonstrate sensitivity. It's a fine line that you need to watch because you're having an impact on that person's confidence and livelihood. When you part company with somebody, there's no need to get worked up and go in with an aggressive approach. This isn't personal – generally, you're doing what's in the best interest of the business. Most people I know find it very difficult to tell people they don't have a job. My Managing Director is one of the few people I know who can handle it like I do. Anyway, Michael took it as well as could be expected and I handed him over to our solicitor, telling him he could ask another lawyer to look at the terms of the exit package if he wanted to. It was all very business-like and amicable.

My father's aversion to this type of conflict extends to his personal life as well. I recall an occasion two years earlier when Dad started dating Lorraine, who was my best friend at the time. It all started off casually enough but then Lorraine started to get a bit too serious and Dad couldn't cope. A few months later he decided it had to end and confided in me that he didn't know what to do. So I sat down and wrote him out a few lines so he had some ideas of what to say. I then sat with him in his office while he called her. Looking back, it was quite funny because Dad was clearly not coping and I ended up mouthing the words he had to say to her. Later on I spoke to Lorraine and she wasn't desperately upset – I suppose she expected it. However, she did comment that when he was speaking to her he sounded exactly like me!

Of course, we disagree but I think that's because we really respect each other and value what the other one has to say. I have learnt an enormous amount from my father's wealth of experience and unconventional style. In turn I believe he has learnt much more about the importance of communicating and structure from me. In many ways we are so similar and where we are not we seem to have a balance of qualities and skills that complement each other. I have tested his patience outside the boardroom, namely at the football. I did not attend my first football game until the autumn of 1998. He is passionate about the game and about Birmingham City, of which he is Chairman. One day he suggested I come with him. We were sitting in the Directors' box and Dad, as usual, was focused on the game, though this was being made slightly difficult by the barrage of questions I was asking. 'Why is he kicking it back the other way?' 'What has the umpire blown the whistle for?' I was desperate to know what I was watching and I think Dad was desperate for me to be quiet, but he patiently answered all my questions. I am an insatiably curious person and will always ask as many questions as I require in order to understand something. However – and I'm not bragging here – I did not need to have the offside rule explained more than twice before I understood. These days I really enjoy football, not just because it's in the family, and I would happily go to watch any other club play if invited.

I love my father and am extremely proud of him. Unlike me, he didn't have the support of his father; in fact, quite the opposite, really. Despite this, Dad has risen above all the challenges life has thrown at him to become one of the most successful men in the UK. There have been low points in my career when my father has reassured me, saying, 'There is nothing to fear but fear itself.' He has always been my rock, the person to turn to when I needed that extra encouragement. Above all he is someone I always knew would be truly honest with me, even if it wasn't what I wanted to hear. He has always had great belief in me and I am only glad that I have been able to live up to it.

CHAPTER ELEVEN

Dates and disasters

I like dating. I like the idea of meeting different people and going out for dinner or drinks, and just getting to know them. I'm not one of these people who expects romance or even a passionate evening from every date. Having said that, I am very selective and my friends even think I'm too fussy. I get frustrated by this as everyone has a flavour or type they prefer and I don't think there's anything wrong with being focused on what you like. I don't want to compromise. I also have so many exciting projects and opportunities, and he would have to be very special to drag me away from all the things I'm enjoying at the moment.

After I'd split up from Ben and finished with Paul, I did what a lot of women do: I went out with my friends, mostly with Carole. Carole was also single and we had a ball going out together and just having a good time. It was a new experience for me as Carole was my first truly close friend and it was the first time I really shared that 'girls, we're in this together' kind of feeling that I imagine many women have enjoyed for much of their lives. Early in 2000 I met Toby Anstis, the DJ and presenter. Soon after I'd bought Knickerbox, Toby decided to run his breakfast show from the window of the Knickerbox store in Kensington. We had a bed in the window and when I turned up at the store we got into bed together and he interviewed me. Toby had mentioned to my publicist, Ghislain Pascal, that he'd love to go on a date with me. I was newly single and a bit out of touch with the dating thing but I thought Toby was lovely and it would be good fun.

Toby is a very warm, friendly person and a true gentleman – but he is also a bit accident prone. On our first date he accidentally threw a glass of wine over me. On our second date we went to the cinema and he tipped a bucket of popcorn into my lap. On the third date we went to Richmond and he nearly got me killed crossing the road. As lovely as he was, I didn't want to risk the prospect of being struck by lightning or having something drop on me from a great height, either of which could be serious possibilities when dating Toby!

Then I met the Flip Flop man. I gave him that name on the basis of one exasperating date – and, no, it doesn't have anything to do with sex! His name was Paul and he was gorgeous, but he was was a little overawed by who I was and what I did for a living. When he found out, he didn't know how to react and didn't quite know how to talk to me.

One time we were due to go to the Atlantic Bar and he rang me and said, 'Look, I've had an accident playing hockey and I've injured my foot. I'm on crutches. Do you still want to go out or rearrange?' I reassured him that crutches were fine. He turned up without them, which was not a good look and meant that when he walked he dragged the injured foot behind him. I was not impressed. After we'd been at the Atlantic we ended up walking in the direction of Leicester Square. It was agonising to walk with him and I kept wishing he'd brought the crutches. When we got to the traffic lights near the Trocadero he said, 'You'll never guess what has happened.' I was not surprised to hear that the shoe on his injured foot was damaged: half of the sole had come away – hence the title of Flip Flop man! Undaunted, I told him that we could go into the Trocadero and buy some trainers so he could throw away the shoes. He refused my suggestion point-blank, saying he did not want to dump his shoes. No, he would find some Superglue and fix them. We then had to spend ages looking everywhere for Superglue. We didn't find it. And I didn't go out with him again.

I am a generous person so naturally I like men who share my values and ideals. That does not mean they have to have as much money as I do but in some way its nice to be made to feel special. On a date I will offer to pay half. Most guys don't accept on the first date, preferring to pay themselves, and then I will usually say, 'Well, I'll get the next one.' I am happy to adapt to situations and have no hard and fast rules, only that I don't like men who are penny-pinching. Recently I went on a date with one such person. My friend Val had set me up with an actor. I was wary at first because he said he had a beard and I am not a fan of facial hair, preferring a clean-cut, smooth look (designer stubble excepted). He told me over the phone that he'd had to grow a beard for a part in a film so he had no choice. I hate to sound shallow but the beard was worrying me; however, I don't like disappointing people so continued with the date. He wanted to meet at the Mandarin Oriental for a drink and I thought that was a good choice. By the time I saw him he had at least trimmed the beard and it looked OK.

He asked me what I'd like to drink so I asked for a glass of champagne. I don't drink fast so it's not like I drink vast amounts. As we were talking I mentioned I'd sent my driver, Brian, away because I didn't want him to know about the date. Brian is very professional and confidential but I guess I wanted to keep it private. After that we jumped into a cab and went to a restaurant in Fulham. By this time I was quite hungry and looking forward to my meal. Almost as soon as we sat down, he said, 'I'm not into dessert because I don't have a sweet tooth.' I told him that was fine and I wasn't that fussed about sweets either. He then said, 'I'm not having a starter. I'm not into them, either. Are you having one?' Well, I hadn't come all this way for one course, so of course I was having a starter. In fact, I'd already spotted what I was having. By now I had detected little signs of frugality. The next thing, his phone rang and he took the call. I heard him on the phone saying, 'Thanks, thanks.' Thinking it might be something to do with an acting part I asked who it was and he said, 'Oh, it's my mum wishing me good luck for the date!' This was not turning out to be a good date.

There was worse to come when the bill arrived. Anyway, when I offered to pay half he didn't hesitate. Quick as a flash he said, 'Yeah fine, that's great.' Without further delay, he proceeded to divide the bill *exactly* down the middle. It came to £64.42 and it took him a while to work out that it would be £32.21 each. I was flabbergasted, not by his slow maths but his tightness. I took £40 in cash from my bag and put it on the table. 'I like a woman with cash,' he said. He wanted to put exactly half on his card and went to great pains to explain this to the waiter, who was looking more embarrassed than I was. When the waiter returned with the change for me, I picked it up and put down a ten-pound note for the tip. 'What are you doing?' he demanded. 'That's your money.' 'I know,' I replied. 'I'm leaving a tip.' He said it was far too much and he'd already paid the tip but I hadn't seen anything except a few measly coins. I left the tip anyway.

Clearly an opportunist, he asked if I was calling my car. I told him I was and it would probably take me at least an hour and a quarter to get home from Fulham. He asked if he could have a lift to Green Park and, not having a great sense of where we were, I asked him if it was on the way. He said it was. When my driver came, he said it was in the opposite direction but we drove him there and got rid of him. While I have no desire to see him ever again, I certainly don't harbour any ill feelings towards him.

The same cannot be said of another man whom I had a lucky escape from. It all started in October 2006 when he contacted me through my publicist, Ghislain. He worked in the City and apparently he'd been to school with my cousin Bradley. He also said he had shared a kiss with me many moons ago. Once Ghislain had passed the email on to me I realised that he'd actually kissed my cousin Tina, so I replied to him saying that he had the wrong girl. A series of amusing exchanges ensued during which he made self-deprecating remarks about always getting the wrong girl. I was amused and a little bit charmed. My sister Vanessa was far more pragmatic: 'Jaq, he will be ugly. Nobody can be that funny *and* good-looking.' She said I shouldn't even bother thinking about it. I should know better than to ignore my sister's advice, but I did, and carried on communicating with him. He sent me another email and asked me if I would sponsor him on a charity event. I tried to help but he confessed it was just an excuse to contact me again. He had such an amazing sense of humour, the type that makes you laugh out loud, and I was really warming to him. Around the same time, I met up with my cousin Tina at my grandmother's funeral. She remembered him and so we sent him a text from my phone – which meant he now had my number. One Friday night I was at home catching up on all those episodes of *I'm a Celebrity* that I'd missed, when he texted. He asked me if I'd like to see a picture of him. I said that would be good. He then said, 'Naughty or nice?' I said 'Both,' and then, realising that could have consequences, quickly texted, 'Nothing that will make me blush.' Ten minutes passed by and I was getting a bit worried. The next thing I knew I had received a picture of him. Not his face or even his head, but his naked torso. Why had he sent it? A few minutes later, obviously after waiting for me to react, he sent a further text asking, 'Have you cum yet?' I suddenly felt ill. I texted him and said, 'You have just gone from funny to sleazy. Sorry, but you have got the wrong girl.'

He replied saying, 'There is a fine line … I have just crossed it. Sorry.' Meanwhile he had sent a facial picture of himself and I realised my sister was right. The next day I still felt disturbed about what he'd done. I had deleted his texts and wanted never to hear from him again. While I was in the car on my way to London, he sent me a text, trying to blame me for what had happened. I ignored it so when that didn't work, he got bitter and wrote, 'I've been with the wrong girls for the last thirty years.' I felt like I'd had a very lucky escape.

CHAPTER TWELVE

The real thing at last?

I like a party. Whether it's my own or someone else's, I love big occasions where everyone goes to a lot of trouble to dress up and gets into the spirit of things. In 2000 I held an Arabian Nights birthday party to celebrate my fortieth birthday. It was to be at my father's home, The Chalet. As well as my close friends and family, guests included Sid Owen, Lucy Benjamin, Steve McFadden, Dean Gaffney, Michael Greco, Toby Anstis, Barry Fry and his wife Kirsty, Ron Noades and his wife Novello and Jasper Carrot, who arrived in spectacular style in his helicopter.

The decor was absolutely beautiful. We organised everything through an events company who put a massive Bedouin-style marquee over the entire patio area which showed off two stunning water features on either side of the dance floor. The whole feeling was everything you would imagine of the Arabian Nights, with rich, over-sized cushions and jewelled accessories. The draped ceiling represented a starry night and there was even a statue of a camel. All the waitresses were dressed as belly dancers as they greeted guests with cocktails. The girl band Fierce performed a number of their hits and even Sid got up and sang along with his friend Lonyo. We laid on courtesy buses to and from the Selsdon Park Hotel, where many guests were staying, and valet parking for the guests that drove. I wore an amazing Neil Cunningham creation, a black fitted dress and Manolo Blahnik shoes.

It was lovely to see everybody. My sister was there, looking radiant, partly because she is beautiful but also because she had dumped Steve after ten years and had got together with Nick, a policeman whom I instantly liked. Seeing him and my sister together, I knew they were just right for each other. Nick would eventually become my brother-in-law, but in the meantime he had added some extra excitement to my birthday by bringing a friend with him who was absolutely gorgeous. Actually he wasn't just gorgeous; if a man can be beautiful, that was how I'd describe Dan. He had dark hair and blue eyes. His was a face that you just wanted to gaze into. I went over and met him, and I was blown away by his infectious smile and warm and friendly personality. There was definitely electricity between us. However, nothing happened that night because I was the hostess and I was making sure all my guests were having a good time.

My sister and Nick went out with a group that included Dan and, as I was single, I often joined them so we saw a lot of each other. It was so obvious that there was a major attraction between us. By now there was lots of flirting going on but he wasn't making a move. I think we were both conscious of the age gap between us, seventeen years, which obviously concerned me, but Dan seemed older than his years and intellectually we were on the same level.

I normally prefer men who are just a few years younger than me. I live a younger lifestyle than my age and a lot of men in their mid-forties would be on a different wavelength to me. I like younger men because they have more energy, like to have fun and are open-minded about everything, not just sex. The only thing I would say is that a date is a date until it becomes something else.

That was about to happen when Dan and I went with the others to the Glasshouse in April 2001. We had our first real kiss there. At the end of the night he offered to give me his phone number so I could 'call him'. I said, 'No, Dan. If you want to take me out, you call me.' I wasn't going to start making the running. Clearly, he'd never had to make much effort before, but he did call as I hoped he would.

Our first date was the best first date I've ever been on. We chatted and laughed all night. It was so natural – you know when you're with someone and you don't have to try to have a good time, it just happens. We started the night off in a bar with champagne. We then decided to move on and went outside to look for a cab. It was proving impossible to find one. A man with a Rolls-Royce pulled up and said he'd drive us where we wanted to go for seven quid. He wasn't a cab driver, it was just a fluke. We went from bar to bar and we were out for hours. In fact, we'd met at six in the evening and didn't get back until four in the morning. Dan couldn't believe that we were out that late, partly because he knew I'd just had an operation on my knee, but neither of us wanted the night to end.

Our relationship began to grow and develop. At that time Bob Latchford, a former Birmingham City footballer who'd also played for England, called me to ask me out on a date. Trevor Francis' wife, Helen, had given him my number. But I'd already started seeing Dan and we were smitten with each other. My concerns about the age difference were fast disappearing. The fact that we had a seventeen-year gap had not particularly worried me but Dan, being just twenty-five, had given me some food for thought, namely, 'Was he ready to commit to a relationship?' We very quickly got past that when it became clear that we were both serious about each other. Dan's main concern was what other people thought. He worked as a trader for a City bank and he got quite a lot of stick from his colleagues. Although, like many women today, I didn't – and still don't – look my age, but my public profile meant that people knew how old I was. Dan really didn't know how to handle the comments about my age, which upset me simply because if the same people had made derogatory comments about his family he would have come right back at them. I don't think he quite knew what to do.

The initial phases of a relationship should be wonderful and our first two years were. In fact, it was effortless. We both enjoyed going out with our friends and throwing dinner parties. We were also fortunate in that, because of Vanessa and Nick's relationship, we shared the same group of friends. I was so happy and in love. And I really felt that this man was the one I was going to be with. With Dan came the bonus of his family. When I met his parents, they were so warm towards me and it felt like I was part of something that I hadn't experienced in my own life. They made me feel very welcome. His mother Lyn was absolutely adorable, a bubbly lady who would do anything for you, and her presence ensured the atmosphere was a warm one. I loved her to bits. I also liked his dad, Roger. He was some-body who seemed to epitomise the best qualities of a family man. You just felt he was there for everybody. Christmas made me feel especially privileged to know them. Lyn held the best Christmas gatherings at her house and, again, it was something I'd never had when I was growing up. I'd go round there and immediately I was embraced by this close-knit family, with dogs barking and a real fire crackling away. It just felt so good to be part of that.

Dan always said he wanted to have a family. Although I've always wanted to have a family, I've never been broody, as I believe being with the right man takes priority. I guess that's why I was biding my time. I was very grateful for my life, and my attitude was reasonably relaxed. I thought, well, if I do have a family it would be wonderful but if I don't I will, of course, be sad but you cannot always have everything in this life. Sometimes it is better to focus on the wonderful things that you do have. While I knew I could afford to support a child on my own, I was of the opinion that a baby should have a father around and I would not get pregnant without having a partner who would be actively involved. This was the first time in my life I had entertained the thought of having a child. I loved Dan and our relationship was a stable one. So I decided to come off the Pill. We were both excited at this new phase in our lives. At the same time we made plans to move in together.

I was still living in Caterham when we met and we would spend about equal time between my house and the new house Dan had just bought in Bexleyheath. We had been looking around for a few months and finally decided on a lovely old barn in Westerham, Kent. It was Dan who spotted the details when they came through and we drove straight over to have a look from the outside. When we first saw the house, it was a bleak, dark, winter night. It was pouring with rain and very windy, but even in the worst weather conditions we could see it was just what we were looking for. We went back to visit at the weekend with the estate agent. It was delightful, with oak beams and unusual features giving character to every room. It was newly converted so there were no changes that desperately needed to be made to the inside. The biggest problem was the garden: it appeared to be invaded by moles. There were mole hills everywhere. It had a beautiful flint stone listed wall running round it and through the middle, which created a secret garden. The main feature was the large natural pond with about four weeping willows hanging over it. Already there were two resident wild ducks that had set up home there. Although I had more funds than Dan, we made sure we structured the purchase so it was fair. If you're moving in together then I think it is important that it is a wholehearted commitment. You both need to feel you have a stake in the relationship, so it was important to me to ensure that Dan felt our house was as much his home as mine. We picked up the keys in May 2002. It was all very stressful as the builder was threatening to pull out at the last minute in the hope of getting more money for the sale. We called his bluff and moved in as planned. Moving house is exhausting so we had little energy for celebrating on the first night; we were just happy to be in the house we wanted so much. We did hold a fabulous Barn Warming party about a month later. We invited all our friends and family and, of course, our new neighbours. The Barn is one of four houses, including an oast house and a lodge. Ashton and Mark, who live in the main house, gave us a fascinating perspective on the history of our properties which at one time formed one estate. Apparently, many years ago it was used as a courthouse where many people were tried for their crimes. The hanging tree at the back of Ashton and Mark's house is still there today!

When a couple decide they want to start a family, they step on to a treadmill from which it is very hard to get off. Suddenly that is all you can think about, especially at certain times of the month. You watch anxiously, thinking, 'Will this be the month that my period doesn't come and I find out I am pregnant?' It had been about nine months and nothing had happened. Every month Dan would ask me if I had started my period. I was beginning to dread telling him because I just couldn't bear the look of disappointment on his face. While I was characteristically positive about things, Dan lost heart very quickly. That side of his character was eventually to create problems for us.

Dan's anxiousness did not help me; in fact, his constant questioning every month was making me feel very pressured. Finally I said to him, 'OK, let's go and get tested so we can see if anything is stopping us from having a baby.' We went off to see my doctor, who referred us to the best consultant she knew, Miss Hannah. The tests were due back a couple of weeks later. Since Dan was too busy at work I went on my own to get the results of our tests. I was quite relaxed as I sat down in the doctor's office. I knew I could conceive because I'd got pregnant when I was with Paul. Since I was forty-two at the time, I was convinced that it was going to be something to do with my age. The consultant told me that I had the eggs of a thirty-two-year old, which was very good news.

I asked her what she thought the problem was and her response was that sometimes these things happen and there is no rhyme or reason. Despite advances in medical science, having a baby is still full of mysteries. She suggested that we might consider IVF if we wanted to improve our chances. I went home and told Dan what the doctor had said. He was understandably disappointed. I was still very positive and tried to reassure him that it was nothing to get down about. 'We can still try. It will just be a different way of having a baby and it will be more special.'

According to the National Institute for Health and Clinical Excellence (NICE), apparently about one in seven couples in the UK have a problem getting pregnant. Within this group, some cases remain unexplained while others may be due to factors such as low sperm count or damaged Fallopian tubes. Today all women who are unable to conceive naturally are able to have at least one cycle of treatment paid for by the NHS, if, of course, they qualify. If a woman cannot afford to go private and pay in the region of £5,000 or so for further cycles – which most women cannot – then she literally has one last chance, which is not enough, as it usually takes on average three attempts at IVF to conceive.

Dan accepted the idea of IVF and wanted to start imme-diately. I wanted to wait a bit but he was piling on the pressure. I wanted to put it off for a few months until January 2003 because I had other things to deal with. Vanessa's wedding to Nick was coming up in November 2002 and I had a hen night to organise, among other things. Dan did not want to wait. He seemed even more anxious than before. 'OK,' I thought, 'this is a pretty tall order but I can do it.' I returned to the hospital – it was the Chelsfield Park Hospital in Kent – and told them we would like to proceed with IVF treatment straight away. Now the phrase 'straight away' is somewhat misleading since there is a hell of a lot you need to go through before being deemed appropriate for the treatment. As you might expect there are endless forms to fill in and criteria you need to satisfy, including letters saying that you would be suitable parents. As if couples wanting to conceive were not already in a state of anxiety! And they are then placed under additional stress by the process. I'm not saying that it's wrong to have a list of criteria – of course, there has to be – but, like most things, it could be improved and made a lot more user-friendly and supportive. Then there is the absurdity of the fact that an irresponsible teenager can get pregnant while adult couples have to have the approval of a cast of thousands. It just doesn't seem right.

There is very little that truly overwhelms me but it's fair to say that this did. It wasn't just the form filling, it was also the hype that came with it. The practitioners are obligated to make you aware of certain risks, necessary in any medical procedure. What annoyed me was that they would tell you about something awful that might happen and scare you, and then you would find out later that the chances of that occurring were very small. I came out of that initial phase feeling exhausted and I can only sympathise with anyone going through it today. Having put pen to acres of paper and provided details of our lives to so many people, we were ready to start the treatment. However, with every-thing going on in my life I was so stressed out that I scared my period away and we were not able to commence IVF until I had my period. I had always been so regular and naturally my first thought was that I might be pregnant. I wasn't. After all that, January would be our start date.

CHAPTER THIRTEEN

Vanessa hitched, Tracy ditched

Vanessa's wedding was held on 23 November 2002 at Highclere Castle in Newbury, Berkshire. It was an exquisite setting and although it was a cold day the sun shone, and so did Vanessa. She wore a traditional wedding dress, designed by Caroline Castigliano, in ivory satin with a ruched bodice and full skirt, and was truly a gorgeous, radiant bride. One of the things that adds to Vanessa's beauty is that she is so unaware of how lovely she looks and to me that makes her even lovelier. Nick and she are made for each other and I was literally overwhelmed with emotion when they walked down the aisle. I did a reading at the beginning and then, once the formalities were over, the party started. The style and elegance of the occasion was, however, lost on a woman called Tracy. Tracy worked for us, as PA to my Managing Director Julie Harris, and had been seeing my cousin Bradley, who also worked for the Gold Group. The idea of her and Bradley surprised everyone since he was rather quiet and conventional and she was a lively girl from New Zealand who had travelled the world and gave the impression that she was up for pretty much anything. I quite liked her. She had spirit and a sense of fun. According to Julie, she took a few liberties in her position but was generally well behaved. Until the wedding, that is.

From the outset Tracy was making the most of her VIP status. She travelled to Highclere Castle with Uncle Ralph and Grandma Rosie, and had plenty of access to good champagne along the way. Following the breakfast, Tracy was a little merry, which progressed to happy, and then euphoric, at finding herself part of such a lavish event. As the evening wore on Tracy became more and more drunk, and by the time the first dance came, there were three people in the marriage – well, three people on the dance floor, to be exact. Slowly but surely Tracy was becoming an unstoppable train, which usually means there's going to be a wreck at the end. It was time for the singer Alexander O'Neal to take centre stage, but, as far as Tracy was concerned, the stage was all hers. Grabbing Alexander's arm, she requested a song, telling him she was his biggest fan so could he please sing it for her? He shook her off, telling her the song was by Luther Vandross. Whoops! It's no exaggeration to say that alarm bells were ringing now and I could see Julie wasn't too impressed. I did manage to steer Tracy away from the dance floor without too much fuss – just in time, since she was about to whizz ninety-

year-old Rosie onto the dance floor. I had visions of poor
Grandma resembling a vacuum cleaner, being shoved
around in a maniacal twirl!

Not surprisingly, Tracy's language took a turn for the
worse and by now she was managing to spill an astonishing
amount of red wine over everybody who was unlucky
enough (or foolish enough) to get near her. At that point I
think Julie stepped in and tried to calm things, suggesting
that perhaps Tracy should have some water. Julie told Tracy
to go home, whereupon she replied that Julie was not her
boss tonight and that she was a VIP guest. Neither Julie nor
I saw her again that night but I heard more about her antics
the following day. For a girl that was completely out of her
tree, she had been busy. After draping herself over Adam
Faith, she moved on to my father, running her hand over his
crotch, stating that my cousin Bradley looked very like him
and asking if he had been a 'naughty boy'. She'd ranted
about Bradley not being senior enough nor respected
enough in the business and discussed his salary with anyone
who would listen. She also told everyone that he was a
bastard. I believe she also used the 'C' word in front of my
father, dropped a glass of red wine that actually exploded on
the floor and managed to get back onto the dance floor for
some wild gyrations. But she hadn't finished. In the car on
the way home – they had a job getting her in there – she
made a pass at the family chauffeur and became very
agitated and aggressive, frightening poor Rosie.

The following day Julie was leaving on a two-week tour of the UK, launching the new Ann Summers catalogue. As her PA, Tracy was meant to accompany her but rang at around 9am, too poorly to attend. At this stage Julie had no idea of absolutely *everything* that had gone on, so when Tracy resigned she did not accept. Tracy joined the tour that night and was, as they say in the tabloids, 'tired and emotional'. The following day Julie heard about all the events and comments Tracy had shared with the assembled crowd the previous night. Not unfairly, she decided Tracy's position was untenable and ordered a taxi for one!

Amid the chaos that Tracy was creating that day and the joy of seeing my sister so happy, I felt uncharacteristically edgy, almost on the verge of panic. Vanessa's wedding had meant I would see my abuser again. I knew he would be there and, as I always did on the rare occasions I saw him, I psyched myself up. This time, however, I was feeling more anxious than I'd ever felt previously. I knew it was down to more than the impending meeting with John. The stress of my forthcoming IVF treatment and all the preliminaries we'd had to go through so far was affecting me. For the first time in ages I was feeling worn out. I was also starting to feel like I was less in control of my life than I had been for a long time. Of course, being me, I didn't dwell on it too much and just got on with what I had to do. As I'd expected, I did come face to face with John at the wedding.

I avoided looking in his direction throughout but his audacity always amazed me. The fact that he'd abused me and knew I didn't want him near me did not stop him coming up to say hello. More than that, he would go to kiss me on the cheek and in one of those Princess Diana/Prince Charles moments, I would turn my head to avert it. With people standing around, it was embarrassing for everybody. Even though nobody, except perhaps my mother, knew the real reason why I avoided him, they were visibly uncomfortable. But their discomfort was minute compared to the way he made me feel.

What I wasn't prepared for was seeing him twice in the same week. I had no idea he would be at my Aunt Marie's sixtieth birthday party a few days later, otherwise I would not have gone. When he walked in and I saw him, my heart started pounding, and I suddenly felt very ill and weak. My whole body felt like I was being prodded by needles and my nerves were so on edge. I suppose this is what they mean by your skin 'crawling'. My chest was hurting and I went hot, then cold. I later found out I was having a full-on panic attack. If you don't know what it is, you're likely to think you're having a heart attack. For some people the attacks happen quite frequently and can be so debilitating they are unable to function in their day-to-day lives. For me there was a definite feeling of loss of control and I asked Dan to take me home. Dan did not understand the severity of my reaction, but instinctively knew that something was seriously wrong and we left the party early. That night I did what I had avoided doing for years: I told him about my abuse. It was the first time I had ever told anyone properly and once it was in the open I told Vanessa as soon as she got back from honeymoon. It was hard because I thought Vanessa was fully aware from the things I had said over the years, but in reality she had no idea of how bad it really was. Dan's reaction was completely different to what I had expected. He was, of course, shocked but so understanding and wonderful. He was also incredibly upset and angry for me and wanted to go over to Mum's house and confront John there and then. This was the first time someone had shown they wanted to protect me. For so long I had wanted someone close to me to understand my pain. Dan is not a violent person but I knew from his anger that if John had walked in the door at that moment he would have beaten the hell out of him. For the first time I felt my feelings had been validated.

We were able to look forward to and enjoy another cosy Christmas with Dan's family and then, in January, it was time for my first IVF treatment. Prior to the treatment it was suggested we see a counsellor who specialised in talking to couples undergoing IVF, apparently all part of the process. Initially neither Dan nor I saw the benefits in doing this, but we were keen to do the right thing and we were put in touch with someone. I wasn't sure what we were expected to talk about but it didn't matter since it was a thoroughly demoralising experience. In my view the counsellor was useless. Actually she was worse than useless: she totally lacked empathy and showed very little interest in how we were feeling. She seemed to have her own agenda, and her method of questioning (or what passed for counselling) was verging on adversarial.

Understandably, we were both anxious but we went into the session thinking that we would be in the care of someone who was accustomed to dealing with that. To this day I cannot understand what she was hoping to achieve when she asked me, 'What is it about being over forty that bothers you?' Dan and I just looked at each other and he held my hand, as if to reassure me. I told her that I didn't have a problem at all. I just could not understand where that question had come from since nowhere along the line had I expressed any concerns about my age. 'Well,' she said, 'it bothers most people so why wouldn't it bother you?' I told her it didn't. By this time I was starting to feel upset but I remained calm. I told her that my age had never bothered me and that I felt good about being forty-two, not just emotionally but physically as well. She seemed to want to go on the attack and said, 'You're very intense aren't you? I want you to know you don't intimidate me, Jacqueline.'

I was shocked. I hadn't tried to intimidate her. I had not brought up the subject of my age. When she had raised it, I had said clearly that it was not a problem. I took a deep breath and told her that she must find me intimidating, otherwise she wouldn't have said that. I wondered whether she knew who I was and was behaving aggressively as a result of preconceived ideas she had about me. I also took the opportunity to remind her that she was supposed to be the expert. I was just a mere patient. She was really agitating me now but she seemed determined to persist in a condescending and unhelpful manner. Turning her attention to Dan, she asked, 'How does it feel to be a failure?' I was appalled and suddenly felt very protective of Dan. 'How can you say that? He's not a failure. What are you trying to do?' The end of the appointment came and she actually had the nerve to try and book another one. We declined and walked out.

We were both very upset. Rightly or wrongly, people like doctors and counsellors occupy an elevated place in society. Their behaviour should be of the highest standard but sadly it often isn't. Again I thought about all the other couples who had to go through this. For many this would be the first time they had really put themselves on the line in their lives, exposing their emotions to others. If they were going to meet with the response I'd had, I despaired. As I've said earlier, it's my view there are many deficiencies in the way the whole IVF process is handled. The discussions rarely mention the pressure it can place on a couple's relationship. It's something that should be addressed. Couples need to know that they may end up questioning everything about their relationship, a relationship that was probably looking very solid before they started. They will dissect their reasons for having IVF and their reasons for being together. Both individually and together they will find that hope can quickly give way to despair. If they are lucky and can maintain their perspective, then they will survive, regardless of whether or not the IVF works. If not, well, they could end up in even greater despair.

While we were waiting for the results of the IVF treatment, I received a rare telephone call at home from John. He told me that Mum had been coughing up blood so he'd called an ambulance to take her to Bromley Hospital. He didn't sound particularly concerned; in fact, he was very dismissive of her, saying that she was being silly since it was only a bit of blood. He wasn't going to the hospital and would let the ambulance take her instead. I called Vanessa and we both rushed to the hospital. Mum was very quiet and nervous. She looked so scared and vulnerable.

Four years earlier, in 1999, we had gone through a similar scenario which also began with Mum coughing up blood. Then it had turned out she had a stomach ulcer. After giving birth to Vanessa, Mum contracted rheumatoid arthritis which had gradually caused her hands and feet to become deformed. The doctors had prescribed the drug Voltarol and it's likely that her long-term use of this may in turn have caused the ulcer. While she was in hospital, the ulcer burst. Mum lost a lot of blood and nearly died. She was in intensive care for three days and I don't think Vanessa and I realised how close we were to losing her. Mum was terrified of hospitals and needles, and you even had to coax her to visit a GP.

Yet even that did not account for her strange behaviour while she was recovering from the ulcer. She would suddenly start talking nonsense, saying things like, 'I went down the river today and had a picnic.' Another time she looked around the ward and asked, 'Who are those strange men over there?' 'They're not men, Mum, they're female patients.' Back then she would become very agitated and confused. I had to spend time talking to her and calming her down so they could give her injections. One night she completely lost control and ripped out all her tubes and her catheter. It was horrible. I asked the doctor why she was behaving so strangely and he said it might be a consequence of the blood transfusion. I didn't buy that. There was much more going on. Looking back, what we were witnessing was the beginnings of senile dementia. It's not something you immediately think of, especially as she was only in her early sixties. It is, however, common in people who drink a great deal. What we didn't know at the time was that Mum had been drinking up to three-quarters of a bottle of gin a day, which over time would have contributed to her early dementia. We didn't realise she had been drinking so much until the doctor asked if she was a heavy drinker as she had the shakes. After that period in hospital for the sake of her health, Mum's doctor advised her to stop drinking. Mum immediately gave up, which shocked us but we were also very proud of her.

Now we were here again, waiting to find out what was wrong with our mother. I'd been waiting for what seemed like hours with Mum while she was initially being examined, when Vanessa suddenly rushed in to warn me that John was at the hospital and was on his way up in the lift. I immediately panicked and ran out of the room in the opposite direction to where we came in. I managed to find another way out. I would go to any lengths to avoid my abuser. Meanwhile, Mum would be having more tests. It looked like it might be something more than a stomach ulcer this time.

Not long after we received the news of Mum's illness, we found out that our first IVF attempt had failed. Dan became very down about it. It was awful hearing the news but I remained positive about our future chances. He was taking it very hard and I remember him saying to me one day, 'If it wasn't for your age we would be fine.' I was very hurt by his remark. I said it wasn't about my age, reminding him that the doctor had pronounced my eggs in excellent condition. I told him that was just the way it was. Life cannot always be explained and trying to create a new life even less so.

Dan's inability to cope with adversity was possibly a result of him having led a reasonably charmed life. He was lucky enough to be born with good looks, he was part of a loving, secure family who had always paid him lots of attention and his dad was the sort of person who sorted things out and smoothed the way. He had a good job, he'd had no problem with meeting attractive women and, up till now, life had been good to him. He didn't know what it was like to fight or struggle for anything and he was finding it hard to cope with this challenge. It may sound like a cliché but it is also true that when you have been through adversity, it helps you appreciate the good things in life. Even with all the success I had, I would still wake up and look around my bedroom and think, 'I'm so lucky being in this beautiful house.' Dan found it frustrating that he could not be the same way and would simply say, 'I can't feel what you feel about life. I wish I could but I don't know how to.' Dan's comment about my age severely knocked my confidence yet I was still making allowances for him. In effect, I was making excuses for him and trying to protect him. I knew I was naturally more positive so I tried to compensate for him not being the same way. It wasn't as if I wasn't hurting too and he was the only one going through it but I suppose it's the way with women – we continue to give support even when we're crying out for it ourselves.

I think Dan was doing his best – in the only way he knew how – to cope with things, and in the middle of what had been a hellish start to the year, he decided to take me away for Valentine's weekend. We were awaiting the results of the tests being done on Mum so things were very tense indeed. Perhaps a weekend away was just the tonic we needed. Dan did things properly and he took me to Bath, where we stayed at The Royal Crescent Hotel. The hotel was luxurious, but in an elegant, understated way, and it had everything you could possibly want for a romantic weekend. At one point several months earlier he'd asked me if I wanted to get married or go for IVF treatment first. I said we should do the IVF first. I don't know why but for some reason I had this thought that Dan was taking me away to propose to me – which he didn't. When we got home I was very disappointed and inwardly upset that he hadn't proposed. Reflecting on it now, I think that one of the reasons was that I was going through such a stressful time, and I just wanted something nice to happen. In the space of a few short months I'd had to endure the hell of seeing John twice, undergone an unsuccessful IVF attempt and some rather indifferent counselling that left me feeling drained and had to deal with Dan's negativity.

And now Mum was dying. We found out she had unspecified cancer and it was raging all through her body. When we first heard the news, Vanessa and I immediately went to see Mum. I remember standing in her kitchen and seeing this terrified look on her face. It was heartbreaking as she looked at me as if to say, 'You have always fixed things in the past, please fix this for me.' I knew for the first time ever I couldn't. There was absolutely nothing I could do.

Vanessa and I decided to take it in turns to go to the house and be with her. We would arrive around nine in the morning, just after John had left for golf, and stay until late afternoon, just before he returned. She needed constant care but John was unhelpful and uncooperative. He resisted having a carer in the house. He was even reluctant to let us put a gate at the top of the stairs to stop her falling. In fact, it was always a battle every time we suggested something that might make her life more comfortable. He would frequently ring Vanessa, ranting and shouting that she was our mother and we weren't doing enough, to which Vanessa replied, 'Yes, she is, but she's also your wife and you're doing nothing.' John's attitude was incredible, considering we had our work commitments and he had recently taken early retirement. He moaned because she was incontinent. He would ring us and say, 'She's starting to smell.' Vanessa and I were beside ourselves trying to work out what to do. We would try to bathe our mum but it was very hard since as she was unable to help herself and she was heavy, like a dead weight. We both had to get in the bath to lift her. John just didn't seem to care about her at all. While he was in the house there were times she would get confused, and managed to wander off down the road on her own, wearing just her nightie, and knock on people's doors. She had no idea where she was and she would say things like, 'Help, I'm being attacked by strange men.' It was terrible hearing all this. One day when Vanessa was at the house she found a bottle of chloroform in the pantry! Not surprisingly, she was worried and rang me immediately. We were both beside ourselves with worry about why this was there, so I rang Mum's sister, Auntie Heather. She told me that when John caught mice he would take them alive from the mousetrap and then snuff them out with chloroform. There was no end to his cruelty. He had to inflict it everywhere.

Despite our persistence, the doctors would not give Vanessa and me the time of day. They only wanted to talk to John, who clearly did not give a damn about Mum. I remember ringing the doctor, feeling anxious and wanting to talk to him. The nurse said he was too busy. 'Can you tell me when he's not busy? I want to talk about Beryl Gold.' I persisted but they didn't want to know. The nurse refused to listen to anything Vanessa and I said about Mum's lack of care at home and actually lectured me, saying, 'You should all pull together in times like this.' I recall the nurse asking me one day, 'Are you talking about your stepfather, John?' I said, no, I was talking about my mum's husband. She kept asking if he was my stepfather. That was how she saw the relationship, but he was not and never will be related to me. I cannot use that word to describe him and I never will.

CHAPTER FOURTEEN

Nowhere left to turn

We were only a few months into 2003 and already it was shaping up to be the year from hell. This is the part that they don't prepare you for when they tell you about IVF – the fallout. The emotional roller coaster of IVF treatment can be a traumatic experience for any couple. With Dan, the IVF appeared to have had a devastating effect on him, even though we'd only been through one attempt. I felt he was becoming detached from me, which also meant that he was unable to see the extent of my feelings. With my mother's illness on top of the IVF result, my anxiety was now constant and it was starting to affect my ability to function. At times the sheer effort of getting up each morning was too much. I could not even be bothered feeding the cats. Getting dressed and brushing my hair seemed to require all the energy I had for the day. I didn't know what was wrong with me but I realised that I had to protect my business, so it was then that I took the step of promoting Julie Harris to

Managing Director. Julie had been with me for nineteen years and she is absolutely brilliant. Naturally, she grasped the opportunity with both hands.

In the meantime I had been looking for ways to allay my anxiety and had spent some time doing yoga to calm me down, but the truth was that I was too far gone for that. I didn't realise it then but I'd already crossed over into a place from where, often, the only way is down. I suppose my natural philosophy in life is to just get on with things no matter what, but the downside is that you ignore what your body is telling you. I saw my doctor and told her that the anxiety and panic had become overwhelming and all I wanted to do was sleep. I didn't tell her the full story about John and my abuse so I don't think she really understood what was happening. After a couple of visits she recommended I go and see a woman called Helen, who was a therapist.

After an initial discussion, Helen felt that I was struggling to express anger at the time; both at Dan and also at my abuser, whom I managed to tell her a little about. She decided the best thing was to regress me and, being totally desperate for anything that might help, I agreed. But it was definitely the wrong thing to do at the wrong time. Suddenly it was like being back in the house with John all over again. She took me back to one of the nights my mum went to my grandmother's and my abuser climbed into bed with me. I have since described it to friends as like watching a horror film with me in it. While I was lying there, Helen kept asking me, 'How does that feel?' She actually made me feel much worse. I came out and got into the car but I could not drive for quite a while. I felt shell-shocked. I had palpitations and chronic pins and needles all over my body: I was in a state of panic. It was a living hell and on reflection I imagine an experience like this could be quite dangerous to some people.

In April 2003 Dan and I had our second IVF attempt, which also failed. The distance that was coming between us was now even more pronounced and Dan seemed to be retreating into himself. While I knew Dan adored me, he was so focused on having a baby he couldn't see anything else in his life – despite the fact he had everything. His friends told him how lucky he was to have his job, his lifestyle and me, but that didn't seem to be enough for him any more. I could only conclude that his love for me was conditional: if there was not going to be a baby, there would be no us. From the moment he got the news that we needed to have IVF, he wasn't the same person. We still did things together and we were still having sex but we were no longer close like we'd been at the beginning. It was so sad as we were drifting apart. It made me feel like it was my fault and my emotions were running wild, all over the place.

Looking back at the emails we sent to each other during the day at work, you can see just how much it dominated our lives – the mere fact that we were sending emails about it was bad enough. In one of them I wrote to him, 'Knowing how much you want a family, I am also a realist. I feel that our relationship will go AWOL if things don't happen.' That is exactly what was starting to happen.

On reflection, I think Dan was emotionally immature. His unrealistic expectations of life demonstrated that to me. I used to say to him, 'I wish I could sprinkle some positive fairy dust in your tea.' He would reply that he wished I could, too, yet despite wanting to be positive (or saying he did) he did nothing to help himself. Try as I might I could not turn his negativity into optimism. He had lost his perspective on life. He wanted everything, so he decided he had nothing. It's a destructive path that we can sometimes take, turning our backs on what we already have because we are so focused on what we don't have. I take the attitude that *now* is what matters and I try to make the most of every day. That doesn't just mean work, it means enjoying the company of friends and family and other things that are really important in our lives. You really have to immerse yourself in what you are doing, whether it's trying to finish a task, playing with children or having a drink with a friend. There is absolutely no point thinking about what has gone before – if I had spent time dwelling on events in my past I would not be where I am today. I believe my ability to put things behind me and to extract the most from each day has helped me become successful. I once read a saying – 'The past is history, the future is a mystery and the present is a gift' – and, to an extent, I think that is true. You can only direct life so much. Pinning your hopes on the future to the exclusion of all things, as Dan did, is not healthy. If you are waiting for happiness to find you, you might be waiting a very long time.

Sometimes the future comes too early, as it did when Mum's illness began to savage her body. In June 2003 she died. We had known it was going to happen soon: her cancer was too far gone and had ravaged her in a matter of months, but that still didn't make it easy to accept. It had been a difficult few months, and Vanessa and I were relying heavily on one another. I am sad to say that Dan was not much help. His obsession with having a baby and with his own happiness meant that when I needed him most, I was not getting any support. One evening I was feeling very low and asked him if he could come straight home after work. He replied that he couldn't since he had to be at a retirement party. Nothing I said would change his mind.

Three weeks before our mother died, Vanessa and I took the difficult decision to put her in a home. She was fragile, both physically and mentally, and John wasn't looking after her. In fact, as time went on, he showed even less compassion. We knew Mum did not have long to live and although we were aware that moving someone to a home can make them deteriorate more quickly because of the physical and emotional upheaval of leaving their own environment, we felt that she was in much more danger from John's indifference. We managed to find a nursing home close to where both Vanessa and I lived. It seemed good, there were nurses there and we knew she would be cared for. John was very relieved. He kept saying things like, 'I can't sit here and watch her die,' as if he cared, but we knew it was all about him, not her. Still trying to protect me from having too much to do with John, Vanessa went to the house to help put Mum into the vehicle they had sent for her. I waited down the road and then got in with her. I told her gently that she was just going into hospital for a few tests. We didn't want to frighten her by saying she was going into a home. Her dementia was very advanced by this stage and we were worried that anything could have confused or frightened her even more.

Vanessa and I took it in turns to be at the home with her. We were there pretty much all of the time, except when we went home to sleep. One night in June 2003 they called us to say the time was near. We quickly got dressed and raced to the home to be with her. We sat with her and held her hand. She had lived such a lonely life and there was no way we were going to let her die alone. John did not visit her once from the time she went into the home. In fact, nobody visited her except Vanessa and I and my father, who spent time with her the day before she died. When we arrived there that night she had deteriorated very rapidly. It could have been the dementia talking but she kept asking for my dad. This was the first time I'd experienced death. Nothing prepares you for it, least of all anything you see on television or in the cinema. There they present a scenario where, no matter what illness the person seems to have, they go peacefully and quietly. It all looks very painless. People with terrible illnesses do not die peacefully. They struggle and they gasp for every breath. To watch my mum going through it was harrowing and it is something I will never forget. At one point I tried to cover Vanessa's eyes but she wouldn't let me. Mum died with us both by her side, holding her hand. We sat there in silence at the realisation it was over and that she was gone. For all that had happened in the past she passed away knowing that we loved her. As soon as Dad heard he came up to the home to support us and then sat with Mum on his own for over an hour. We then we had to ring people and tell them. I sometimes wonder what the point was of calling anyone since she did not have any friends visit in her dying days. As far as I'm aware, even Vera, who had been at her wedding, did not come. Without wanting to apportion blame, I don't think Mum was given the correct palliative care. She suffered a lot of pain and had no access to a Macmillan nurse, which she should have had. While the home was good and they had nurses to administer her morphine, there was not enough support in the lead up to her transfer there and it was too late to change things once she'd moved there. We did actually go looking for a hospice at that time but the ones that were close by were all full. I think she slipped through the net, partly because of the way her GP would not speak to Vanessa and me, insisting on speaking to John, who was largely indifferent.

There is no doubt that my mother suffered far more than she needed to – and she is just one of thousands of people who are treated in the same way. I find it extraordinary that we let people go through pain to the very end of their lives, deluding ourselves that they are dying a 'natural' death. There is nothing natural about suffering when you are patently going to die in a few hours or a few days. I would not have said this before having this experience, but now I think sometimes the way we treat the dying is totally inhumane. Sure, there are ethics involved but I have a sneaking suspicion that, like many things in this world, it's not just about that but also about people being too frightened of being sued. I don't have the answers but I do know we all need a better choice than the one we have. On the day Mum died I called Dr Clark, who was responsible for her nursing home in Caterham, and said, 'There must be something you can give her to speed this up.' She was literally crying out.

His words were, 'You wouldn't treat a dog like this, would you?' Until you are right next to them, you don't know how it feels to see someone suffer, to watch them go to the very end attached to a morphine pump – which I desperately wished would speed up. I couldn't bear watching her suffer and, although it may sound shocking to some people, if the doctor had said, 'Here you are, this will help her. I won't do it but you can,' then I would have done it.

Mum's funeral was held at St Mark's Church in Biggin Hill. I was so depressed about everything by then, I didn't shed tears. Mum was dead, I had problems with Dan and I was worn out from depression, although nobody at the time had told me it was that. I just felt so empty and all I could do was hang on, dealing with each minute as it came. Not least listening to the vicar reading the sermon with material John had provided – saying things like, 'She had friends that really cared about her.' Well, she didn't have many friends because he didn't like it unless they were also friends of his, but where were they when she needed them most? He put on such a show at the funeral, walking behind the hearse and pretending to be the loving, bereaved widower.

Grieving Mum was a very difficult process. Normally, when you lose someone you love you take comfort in reflecting over wonderful memories. Sadly, neither Vanessa or I could recall one happy memory to remember her by. My mother was terrified of life and met a man who made her more terrified. He eroded any confidence and self-esteem she had. She lived a totally negative life, one that may have not helped her when her illness came along and possibly made things worse. But she chose him. She had the chance not to choose him a second time, but she did, and it sealed her fate.

CHAPTER FIFTEEN

Putting the government on trial

Serious cracks were starting to appear in my personal life in 2003 but I had some pressing business to attend to with the government which had begun around a year earlier. We'd been advertising Ann Summers job vacancies with JobCentrePlus for some years. In early 2002 I learnt that they were no longer taking our advertisements. JobCentrePlus is part of the Department of Work and Pensions and we couldn't understand the change in policy. Our enquiries revealed that they didn't seem to know why they'd done it, either. It seems that someone in the organisation had suddenly decided that it was inappropriate for JobCentrePlus to continue to advertise vacancies at Ann Summers because we were a 'sex shop'. This is what happens when you have someone who doesn't know what we do – they have their own beliefs and they cannot see past their own preconceived ideas.

I wrote to them, pointing out that we'd had great success

with our placements from them over the years and many of the people we'd hired had risen to managerial positions within the company. Their reply stated, 'We do not accept any job ads for any business related to the sex industry.' I wrote again letting them know that we were not a sex shop because in order to be one, you had to have a license – our shops were not licensed because they did not need to be. Moreover, we had somehow managed to employ about two thousand employees plus seven thousand five hundred sales organisers, including a high proportion of women, none of whom have felt uncomfortable in any way working for us. The response from JobCentrePlus was nevertheless a negative one, so I decided to invite them to come and meet us and see our operation. They duly turned up and we took them to some of our shops and showed them around our building, just as we'd done with the Dublin Corporation. And we introduced them to people who'd been recruited through JobCentrePlus – but it seemed that they'd made up their minds. Like the Dublin Corporation before them, they had their own agenda.

What also became evident is that they'd rewritten their policy so that Ann Summers fell outside their criteria. We decided to get our lawyers involved. They examined the policy and confirmed it was designed to exclude us. I was very angry about this because it meant we were being forced to hire staff through recruitment agencies, a move which could potentially cost us up to £250,000 a year. At the same time jobs were being denied to young people who came through JobCentrePlus. The government, in its wisdom, had decided that jobseekers would be too embarrassed to apply for a job with us. The reality was that the JobCentres had never had a complaint from a jobseeker, nor had any of their staff complained.

Geoff Tyler from Pinsent Curtis Biddle, whom I trust implicitly, said the next step would be to take the case to the High Court. The thought that I could do that momentarily stunned me, but as the idea took hold I realised I had to do it. I suppose it goes back to what I went through in trying to set up a shop in Dublin, and even back in 1985 when I was almost arrested in Bristol. It all feels like bullying and for me that is like a red rag to a bull. I felt that I could challenge this. I knew that taking the case to court would cost money. It would also be a risk to the business because it would focus a great deal of attention on us, but I was confident we would have public opinion on our side because the government was effectively denying work to young people. On Wednesday, 11 December 2002, we issued court proceedings at the Royal Courts of Justice to sue the Minister of State, Nick Brown, and the Department of Work and Pensions. The date for the case to be heard was set: Friday, 16 May 2003.

Arriving at the Royal Courts of Justice is quite a humbling experience – I suppose in many ways these buildings are designed to do just that. The courts are housed in the

Strand, in London, within this magnificent Gothic building which was designed by a man called G. E. Street. The rumour is that the strain of such an enormous project led to Street's untimely death. The building contains over a thousand rooms. Its architecture is very striking throughout and really does take your breath away. The role of this court is to hear some of the country's most serious civil, libel and appeal cases. The public are permitted to view all eighty-eight courtrooms, unsupervised – though judges are quick to reprimand people who try to interrupt proceedings.

So here I am, all 5 feet 2 inches of me (aided by some four-inch heels, of course), walking into this most imposing and formal of buildings.

I am always very interested in what other people do and how they do it, so quite aside from it being my case, I found the whole process fascinating as well. Meeting our barrister was a key moment for me: I needed to know that she actually believed in what we were fighting for. Her name was Kate Gallafent, a young woman whom I immediately respected and who I felt was right behind me. She was brilliant. She argued that we had been allowed to advertise in the past, 'apparently without bringing civilisation to an end'. She made the point that it was unfair to allow other companies, whose jobs could offend certain groups of people, to advertise. For example, would a Jew or a Muslim want to work in a non-kosher or non-halal butcher's shop? There was also the fact that department stores such as Liberty and Selfridges sold sex toys but were allowed to advertise in JobCentres. Kate Gallafent also said that if people were going to get embarrassed surely they would be more likely to be offended if they found a vibrator where they might not expect to, such as in Selfridges, rather than in one of our shops.

The judge was Mr Justice Newman and I saw he had a twinkle in his eye. There was one point during the case when he said, 'But even the downstairs part of the Oxford Street store is non-offensive.' Oh my God, I thought, you've been in there. He'd obviously done his research. I had the distinct feeling that he was a fair man. We didn't get the result straight away so I was on tenterhooks, waiting for almost a month. The judge said we had been singled out unfairly. He said that the JobCentre policy had paid 'insufficient regard to its legal obligation to assist employers and appears to have paid no regard to the potential benefit which jobseekers could obtain by taking up employment with Ann Summers'. He also said it had neglected the possibility that job ads could be accepted in a way that did not lead 'to any significant embarrassment to jobseekers'.

We had won! It was a major moment and one that had no doubt been propelled along by the media. It was also good, knowing public opinion was on my side. I wanted to win because I like winning. But I am also fair and even-handed, and what annoyed me was that the JobCentres broke all the rules on fairness. When you believe so much in something, you want the right outcome. And now I had it.

As we came out of the High Court, dozens of photographers and TV crews were waiting. I gave a short statement to the journalists, followed by a couple of TV interviews with the BBC and Channel 4. Dan was away that day on a golfing trip while family and colleagues were busy with their commitments, so I took Gary Burgham, my Human Resources Director, and the legal team off for some lunch and much-deserved champagne.

Defeating the government was a highlight in what was otherwise a very dismal period. My depression – and I still didn't know for sure if it *was* depression – was getting worse. I was not only going through bereavement, but somewhere I'd had to find the strength to get through my third IVF attempt. In what was a spectacular piece of timing the eggs for the third attempt were collected the day after Mum's funeral. I'd previously asked the doctor if I should postpone it but she said it wouldn't make any difference. I wasn't so sure – how can stress not play a part? After the first attempt we'd moved to the Lister Hospital in Chelsea, regarded as a centre of excellence for IVF. From a personal point of view the overall experience we had at the Lister was much better than the previous hospital, but once again the treatment did not succeed.

While all this was happening, my relationship with Dan

was going downhill; we were not enjoying ourselves anymore. As I'd feared, the desire to have a baby was threatening to split us up. When one thing is wrong in a relationship and it stays around long enough, it tends to dredge up other issues which may have laid dormant otherwise. That was particularly the case with Dan. He later told me that at this point he had started wondering whether he could have a relationship with me without children. He was grappling with the worry that the person he loved might not be enough for him, and was generally beset by negative thoughts and questioning everything. Was Dan looking for problems? I don't know. All I do know is that he'd lost sight of the positives in our relationship, and it was starting to bring me down as well. I tried to help him see the bigger picture but I just couldn't do that *and* look after myself – something I was struggling to do.

I wasn't coping well with Mum's death but, despite my feeling of total despair, I was still trying to help myself, something I have done all my life. I decided I needed to talk to a bereavement counsellor but had no idea who to turn to. Because of my high profile I wanted to be careful whom I approached in case they took advantage of me, so I decided to contact Beechy Colclough. Beechy had worked with a lot of stars like Elton John, Michael Jackson and Kate Moss, so I thought, well, at least he knows about privacy. Beechy had appeared on television, written a number of books and had a good reputation. Or so it seemed. In 2006 he was actually struck from the British Association for Counselling and Psychotherapy list after a number of female patients complained about his alleged behaviour.

However, this was 2003 and he was held in pretty high regard. I was in such turmoil and had no idea how to find him so I called directory enquiries and got his number – and his fax number. I didn't want to call so I wrote him a letter explaining what had been going on and why I wanted his help, and sent it off. I'd included my telephone number so he could phone me and make an appointment. The next day I received a phone call from an unlikely-sounding chap. 'This is Colclough Garages here and we deal in servicing cars.' Shit! Of all the things to happen now, I had sent the fax to the wrong person and told him all about myself, the abuse, problems with Dan and everything. I was absolutely mortified and, to make matters worse, I couldn't get this man off the phone. He just kept on talking, and finally I just apologised and put the phone down on him. I was back to square one.

Dan's behaviour had changed since just before the funeral: he'd started to roll in late and I was getting suspicious about what was going on. Remember, I'd learnt a bit about cheating men from Ben and Paul! One night in early July, just after I'd had the embryos put back in, my curiosity got the better of me and I looked at the text messages on his phone. There was one from a girl called Steph, which was very explicit. His reply to her said, 'You rock.' I was absolutely devastated as I felt the bottom had just dropped out of my world. I immediately woke him and challenged him about it. Naturally, he denied it, but I didn't believe him. The next morning the situation was still unresolved and despite our huge row the night before which meant I was still very upset about the texts, he still went to work. He rang me later that morning to say the girl had explained. She'd made a mistake and sent them to him by error – they were meant for her boyfriend. But that still didn't explain his response to her.

In the following days he orchestrated a series of emails that began with her sending one to him explaining what happened and him sending it on to me. I knew it was staged and designed to substantiate his story, but I couldn't prove it and in any case chose to believe that they hadn't actually slept together. With a not-insignificant sense of déjà vu, I decided to ring her. I'd done this sort of thing before and had absolutely no qualms about doing it again. As I did when both Ben and Paul cheated, I took this course of action because I didn't want to waste time with lies and denials. I wanted to get to the bottom of things and hear it for myself.

The problem was I didn't have her telephone number. I knew she worked in a dealing room for another bank, so I'd have to be a bit clever. I figured out the bank name from an email address I'd seen, so I rang them as if I often did and said, 'Can I speak to Steph, please?' I thought that if I used the shortened form of her name and said I was a friend, I would have some credibility. I did exactly that and they put me through to her. I questioned her and she miraculously had the same story as Dan's. I then asked her if it was true. She said yes, and giggled. In fact, she giggled all the way through the conversation; it was all just pathetic. I felt I'd invested so much in the relationship that I decided to give Dan the benefit of the doubt. We talked – and decided we both wanted to stay together. But over the following weeks we continued in much the same vein as we'd been doing since the beginning of the year, which meant we hadn't fixed anything: we'd only swept our problems under the carpet.

CHAPTER SIXTEEN

Anita: a tragic life

On 16 July 2003 I received an urgent telephone call from Julie Harris. She had taken a call from a man who told her that a friend of his, called Anita, had been the victim of a house fire in Nottingham two days earlier. Apparently, the fire department had told her that it had been caused by her Rampant Rabbit. Anita was a depressive whose eight-year-old daughter had died a year earlier. It was very tragic; the little girl had had a terminal illness, but died prematurely due to hospital negligence. Now all Anita's precious mementos had been destroyed, along with most of her other possessions. She now had nowhere to live, and her friend said Anita and her young daughters and son needed our help. He said they had no contents insurance and the council could only offer them a hostel, which would split up the children and, given the trauma they'd all been through, Anita didn't want to do this. He also said that the *News of the World* had been in touch and wanted to buy their story. It was a lot of information for me to take in; and questions were formulating in my mind.

We contacted the local fire brigade and spoke to an officer who verified that there had been a fire in that area at the time stated. He said the fire had caused severe damage to the upper floor of the house and there were two possible causes: a cigarette butt or a sex toy. His view was that Anita's Rampant Rabbit had been the cause since she had denied smoking in the bedroom, and he could not find any evidence of smoking upstairs. He therefore thought that the cause was the batteries in the vibrator. This was a very unusual situation. We first discussed it with our in-house legal people who strongly advised it should immediately be handed out to lawyers. I didn't agree and felt that, whether it was our responsibility or not, something more had to be done, something personal. I spoke to Julie and we agreed she had to go up there. We wanted to show our support and see if there was anything we could do to help. I also asked her to find out more about the case while she was there.

When Julie arrived she offered to put the family up in a hotel and give them money for clothes, about £2,000 in all. She had instinctively felt that the situation was not wholly above board, but set about attempting to establish a relationship with Anita, something that would be necessary if we were to get to the bottom of this. Anita seemed very concerned that the press had found out about the situation; she had already had calls on her phone from the *News of the*

World and the *Sun*. She told Julie she really did not want to take the money but she was desperate. Julie advised Anita that she would get to the bottom of the matter and would conduct a full investigation, but stressed that she could not understand how our product could have caused the fire.

Julie visited the shell of the burnt house with Anita. She told me how distressing she found it watching Anita searching among the rubble for her dead daughter's belongings and this made her decide to offer to cover Anita's costs in rented accommodation for a period of six months. Meanwhile she'd asked Anita what batteries she had been using in the Rabbit. Anita was very vague, saying it was a silver and red battery; she had one with her and showed this to Julie. Apparently, the Rabbit had been in the washing basket upstairs when the fire started.

Julie then got Anita to agree to give us access to search the burnt-out shell of the house. This was vital if we were going to find out the truth. We first had independent tests done by an inspector from the fire service. His report said he was 99 per cent sure the Rabbit had *not* caused the fire – but, for me, this wasn't good enough. We were talking about doubts being cast upon one of our best-selling products, so what we needed was 100 per cent certainty. I authorised Julie to find the best person she could to investigate the case. By this time I was having increasing doubts about Anita's integrity. There was definitely more than a whiff in the air that someone had put her up to it.

To make things even more complicated Anita said she was pregnant, and hinted that she'd taken tablets to 'lose' the baby. She then began to make all sorts of requests of us, including an overseas holiday. To meet her halfway, Julie offered to send her to Centre Parcs, but this was rejected and she requested a villa abroad, for her family and some friends. However, as passports and birth certificates had been lost in the fire this would prove to be difficult, so Jersey or Guernsey were offered as alternatives. Things got even more bizarre. At one point Anita told Julie that her father was a High Court judge in Ireland. He was very unhappy that she had allowed the Rabbit out of her hands – for the investigations – and was arranging top barristers for her. She wanted Ann Summers to pay for her journey to Ireland and put her up in a five-star hotel. None of the details she gave seemed to make sense, and Julie and I both felt strongly that someone else was behind it. But first we had to prove that our Rampant Rabbit was not the cause of the fire.

In the meantime Julie located the investigator who had examined the evidence from the famous Lockerbie air crash. We couldn't get better than that! I told Julie that whatever he said, I would accept. With Anita's permission, he went to the burnt-out house to carry out his investigations. His conclusion was that she had lied to investigators by saying she didn't smoke in her bedroom, as there was evidence of her smoking in bed and cigarette burns on the carpet. It transpired that she'd taken a phone call at 5am on the day of the fire and had been smoking while she talked. Having also taken the sedative, Temazepam, she fell asleep during the call – and the cigarette caused the fire. As for the vibrator, she admitted to the investigator that it had only one battery in it because she didn't want it to turn on by accident and then go flat. The investigator said that in light of this, there was no way it could have caused the fire. We were provided with copies of his report, detailing the extensive testing that had been carried out on the product and providing the proof that it was an impossible cause of the fire.

In November we received a letter from Anita's solicitors, stating that Anita had not said one of the batteries was removed from the vibrator and confirming they had a copy of the very first report from the fire brigade that showed there was no evidence of the fire being caused by a cigarette. They also wanted the toy sent to them. A few days later Anita rang Julie on her mobile phone in a very distressed state. She said she needed money and she wanted it today; she was talking wildly about having seen an article in the press regarding vibrators and said she had thrown her daughter's ashes in the river. She then became hysterical and wanted confirmation of a £100,000 payment from me or she was going to the press. She said we had tricked her into giving us the product while she was vulnerable. Finally, she started screaming about talking to the *News of the World* and breakfast TV, and hung up.

We knew Anita was depressed but we'd had no idea how severely. Two months passed, and about three weeks before Christmas Julie received a phone call from Anita's sister to advise us that Anita had committed suicide. Julie and I, and everyone who had been involved in the case, were shocked and obviously devastated to hear the news. Julie explained all of the circumstances to her and told her it had been proven that the product could not have started the fire. She was very reasonable and understanding, and said Anita had talked about Julie to her; she was grateful for the help we had given the family. A letter was sent confirming the conversation, and Anita's sister confirmed they were satisfied that the evidence that had been presented to them was correct and that the case would go no further.

However, in April Julie did receive a call on her mobile from a gentleman who identified himself as a friend of Anita's. He asked if we knew that Anita had killed herself due to the stress of the situation following the fire caused by our product. He said he wanted an update with regard to the claim against us. He also mentioned the press. Julie took his number, and our solicitor called him and advised him in no uncertain terms he had no claim. The case was closed.

The fact that none of this turned out to involve Ann Summers in any way was never my main concern. When we first got word of the fire, we had no option but to take the claims seriously – my view is that any business faced with a similar situation needs to do so. Anita's was clearly a tragic situation and you could not help but feel for this woman. Her death reminded me – and should remind us all – that we don't live in a vacuum and that life in all its forms is going on outside our own world. Most of all it was a reminder that for some people every day is simply about survival, nothing more. Anita was not living, she was struggling just to exist. I still get upset when I think about her.

From my own experiences I understood how depression had taken over Anita's life. Some people have described it as a prison and that's exactly how it feels. Unlike unhappiness, you cannot shake it off when you decide to. It stays with you; it goes to bed with you; and it wakes up with you. And while it may start in your brain, it slowly but surely invades your whole body. It makes you tired, it affects your memory and concentration and even your eyesight can be impaired as mine was; and, in a matter of a few weeks, it can turn the strongest, fittest, most motivated person into one that cannot bring him or herself to get out of bed. To all those people who are of the 'just pull yourself together' school, I can categorically state that when you are depressed your brain's chemistry will not allow you to pull yourself together. It just won't work. Prior to my own encounter with depression I was guilty of that way of thinking, but once you've gone down that dark road you know that it's definitely not mere unhappiness. A night out with a friend can help you forget you're unhappy: nothing will help you forget you're depressed. You have to get help. But like a lot of people, I still hadn't got the help I needed because I wasn't aware of the seriousness of my condition, and my GP didn't seem to be either. I hadn't told her about the abuse and my problems with Dan, and so, understandably, she assumed my change in behaviour was all down to Mum dying. At one point she'd given me a very low dose of antidepressants but they didn't do anything for me.

In September I'd somehow managed to do a photo shoot for *OK!* magazine with Dan. There we were in our lovely house, portrayed as the couple who had it all: success, the perfect lifestyle and love. It just makes you wonder how many other people put on a brave face for the cameras. My depression was getting worse but at that point it still didn't have a name.

CHAPTER SEVENTEEN

The roller coaster continues

They say that people are at their lowest during December–January: indeed the Samaritans handle a huge increase in calls over the Christmas period. For me, Christmas 2003 was simply a continuation of the downward spiral I'd been in for pretty much the whole year. I'd now reached a point where I knew I had to do something or else I would fall apart, both physically and emotionally. Exhausted and in despair I went back to my GP who now realised that this was not a case of transient mild depression but something far more serious. She referred me to the Priory Clinic in Hayes, Kent. There I met with a psychiatrist, Dr Sara McCluskey, whom I immediately knew I could trust and who I knew would help me. It took her very little time with me to figure out what was wrong. 'You have Major Depressive Syndrome.' Hearing those words come out of her mouth absolutely stunned me. Of course, I had known I wasn't right but to be told that I had depression and it was very serious was unexpected.

Depression is not just about being very unhappy. It is an actual illness, something I realised when, in a bid to understand it better, I started reading every book I could find on the subject. Like any other medical condition, it requires a strategy. That may mean taking drugs either for a shorter or longer period, often combined with therapy of which there are many different forms. As for the view that 'antidepressants are bad, and have side effects', I have often found this to be the argument of people who have not been there. All medication has potential side effects, but for some reason those of medication taken for a 'physical' illness are deemed acceptable. Antidepressants are not new but the media coverage they get – often adverse – would often suggest they have the same status as some pill peddled by a dealer on the street. Plenty of people take them, and have done so for many years. As a result, they are able to have a quality of life they would otherwise not have. And for some people they are the difference between life and death.

Without wanting to sound like a know-it-all, unless you have suffered depression you simply cannot know what it's like to find yourself in this lonely prison while the world dances around you. You can see and hear what is going on but you're not part of it. It is estimated that more than 2.9 million people in the UK are diagnosed as having depression at any one time. As many as one in five people will be affected by depression at some point in their lives. Some may be cured in months but some may continue to suffer throughout their life. There are no instant cures: antidepressants can take up to a few weeks to start working with your chemistry and even then they do not make you miraculously happy. What they gave me was an ability to function, to be able to get out of bed and get dressed instead of thinking, 'I just can't do this.' Now I had a floor to stand on, I could start rebuilding myself.

I was having regular sessions with a qualified therapist at the Priory, who specialised in counselling victims of sexual abuse. I talked about Dan, about my mother, about the IVF and, for the first time, about the abuse John had inflicted on me. I was finally ready to discuss it. Up till now I'd had no wish to do so. And I now had no choice but to talk about it anyway: I had reached a point where it was time to get things out in the open or my health would continue to suffer. Over thirty years after my abuser began his reign of terror, I was able to release all my feelings and thoughts. It was very painful and tough but it was a huge relief as well. Nonetheless, there was no quick fix and I had a long way to go with my therapy.

Meanwhile the problems that had built up during 2003 were unresolved. With three failed IVF treatments behind us and the gulf between us widening, Dan and I were stuck at an impasse in our relationship. In March 2004 I asked

Dan to move out because I just felt like I was breathing for two people and I could no longer cope. Dan also seemed depressed and the atmosphere had become claustrophobic: that's what happens when you have two people who are feeling damaged. The fact that I'd suggested he leave didn't make it easier. My physical stress symptoms ranged from backache that was so chronic I couldn't sit down, to vomiting. I decided I needed to take myself away and booked a week's holiday in the Caribbean.

I flew off to Barbados and it felt good to be free of worries for a week – relatively speaking. Not long after I came back Dan and I got back together. I wasn't sure about it but he persuaded me things were going to be different. The truth is there was much more love and affection when we were apart. When he returned and got over the pain of missing me, it wasn't long before the possibility of not having children resurfaced.

We lasted about a month before I was feeling the need for space again. I was having enough trouble looking after myself and I just couldn't cope with Dan's constant negativity, which was draining me and was too much of a burden. I decided to escape once more and this time I went to Dubai, taking Dan's younger sister Charlotte with me for company.

Even if our relationship could be fixed I wasn't sure that he was committed enough. I also questioned whether we'd put ourselves into roles that we just couldn't change. The subject came up in greater detail a few months later when Dan left for a third time – his choice. This time I decided that we should have no contact for at least a few months so I could move on. After two months he started sending emails. One of these was asking my advice on what he should do to make things between us right. My reply to him in September 2004 went like this:

I expect my man to look after me rather than the other way around. I don't want to be put on a pedestal. I want to be loved for who I am as a person, cherished and looked after unconditionally. I want my man to be my equal but most importantly to be a real man. A man wouldn't run when things went wrong. He would face the issues and deal with them. I have never felt so abandoned and discarded in my life ... I don't want to replace anyone's mother. I am a woman who wants to feel sexy and confident with the right man, to support him in times of need, but not to make every decision ... It's hard for me to advise you because firstly I am not sure how I feel and also because I just don't want to play that role any more – it's draining and unsexy!

While we were apart I was making a strong effort to get on with my life. I'd been away with Sandie and Vanessa for a girlie weekend in Marbella. I'd also spent a few days in Bordeaux with Carole at Sid Owen's house. I had originally met Sid through Carole after I split up from Ben. We got on really well. Since then it seems that every time I break up with someone I go and stay at Sid's house and he has become a good friend. What I like about him is what you see is what you get. What you saw on *I'm a Celebrity, Get Me Out of Here* in 2005 is exactly how he is in real life, minus the jungle gear. He is a great host, and an excellent cook who produces wonderful breakfasts and a great Sunday roast. He's very well adjusted and not at all pretentious, as some actors are. He has a lovely home in Bordeaux and also owns a restaurant. When we're there it's very relaxed. We watch TV, go shopping and sit in cafés drinking delicious hot chocolates and munching croissants. On this occasion I'd decided to take him an Ann Summers goody bag containing, among other things, a pair of handcuffs covered in leopard print fake fur. He was beaten to them by security at Gatwick airport, who promptly confiscated them.

There were other moments of happiness as well. My friend Carole asked me to be godmother to her son, Ben. I was overjoyed and in August 2004 attended his christening. There I met Joanna, whom I would describe as a cross between Glynis Barber and Meg Ryan, and we became immediate friends. She was both womanly and girlie, with her own highly developed sense of style, often favouring vintage clothes. When I met her she was fifty-one years of age, yet had the most amazing, sexy figure that younger women envied. She also had a brilliant, quirky sense of humour. Joanna would invite us all to dinner and nothing would be prepared. Instead we would be bundled into the kitchen, given loads of champagne and told to cook 'as creatively as possible'. Of course, we would be totally drunk by the time we ate but Joanna pointed out that everything tasted better that way. I called her 'my lucky star'. We had many sunny afternoons in my garden, drinking rosé and eating cake that she'd baked and brought with her. I also appreciated the fact that Joanna had a different perspective from my other friends. When she met Dan, she immediately understood why I had fallen for him. When things between Dan and me went downhill she even offered to talk to him.

At about the same time as I met Joanna, Dan started really begging me to come back. He said he couldn't live without me and he wanted to make a go of it. We would have more IVF and if that didn't work he was willing to investigate other options, even adoption. It had suddenly occurred to him that not having children was not the end of the world, a view I'd always held and still do. I was not convinced of his sudden positive outlook. I wondered whether these were real feelings or simply a consequence of his inability to cope without me. He'd once admitted in an email that the age gap had bothered him – I still had no idea if he'd ever resolved that. Could I cope with the insecurity of being with him again? Would the pain of missing me while we were apart soon pass, only to be replaced once again by the issues that drove him away the last time? I think that, deep down, I knew it probably wouldn't work, and that it had stopped working a while ago – but there was a hopeful part of me that wanted to believe in him.

As we all know, with relationships it's not over until it's over, which means that even when there is just the merest sliver of hope it's tempting to cling to it. I'd actually been doing all right without him. The therapy was going well and I was feeling much stronger. I had a great circle of friends, a full social calendar and a job I was passionate about. My brain said 'no' but my heart said 'yes'. Well, I listened to my heart and Dan came back, full of promises and the mention of marriage. It sounded too good to be true, and it was. But we'd never fixed the things that had undermined our relationship from the start – Dan's negativity, his need for me to take care of things and of him, our differing views on the part children would play in our lives – so we really didn't have a secure basis for going forward. It's a common mistake that lots of people make. Getting back together takes far more effort than getting together at the start, and maybe we didn't have it in us any more. But we had time, something my friend Joanna didn't.

The things that shine brightest often burn out the quickest, and that's what happened to Joanna. In 2005 she was diagnosed with stage four lung cancer. This was a woman who, just before I'd met her, had survived early breast cancer. She'd come through a lot. She'd run a very successful IT company and owned a beautiful house in Sussex. Her boyfriend had not only cheated on her, but had also embezzled

£100,000. After that she became depressed, but she had tried to be positive about things. You would expect nothing less of Joanna. She was an example to all of us.

Joanna was a fighter but her cancer was far too advanced for her to get through it so the emphasis was on extending her quality of life. She handled it all with humour, grace, deep spirituality and her customary sexiness! I remember she had a crush on her oncologist, Bob, and one day when I went to see her in hospital there she was sitting up in bed, hair up like Pebbles from *The Flintstones*, wearing a short nightie and surgical stockings – she could even make those particular garments look sexy!

Sadly, or perhaps mercifully, the end was relatively quick. When she was diagnosed in June 2005 I decided to arrange a photo shoot with my close girlfriends. I'd been wanting to do it for a while but when the severity of Joanna's illness was known I decided to do it as quickly as possible. All the girls were there – Val, Sandie, Carole, my sister Vanessa and Joanna. I had Chris Harding take the photographs and brought in my own make-up artist, Virginia, whom I knew very well. Joanna was very poorly but nevertheless came to the shoot, and we made her feel special. She was sick from the chemotherapy she'd undergone that morning, but once Virginia had transformed her she turned it on for the camera like she always could.

In November 2005, five months after her diagnosis, Joanna went home to New Zealand to die with her family around her. We sent one of the pictures taken on that day and they put it in her coffin. She meant a lot to us and I think of her often. Once we went to this charity auction where I had my eye on a signed book by Salvador Dali and Joanna helped me bid. There was also a hideous painting of a Buddha that she insisted I had to have, and she made me go for it. Now it's in my study at home and reminds me of a beautiful friend who is no longer with me.

It was a period of contrasts. A woman who lived emphatically for the moment, and squeezed everything out of it, had suddenly left us while, not far away, Dan was still trying to work out what mattered in life.

CHAPTER EIGHTEEN

Oxford University requests

I'd been in therapy for over a year now and in that time had worked through all of the problems associated with my past. I had finished the medication I had been prescribed and my therapy sessions were coming to an end. I was no longer anxious or despairing and felt much more like the old Jacqueline again. With that new-found strength, though, came the fear that my world might capsize again if things went wrong. I asked my doctor if I could ever get this low again. She said that it was highly unlikely. She told me that I was an extraordinarily strong woman who had survived things that would break most people. It had been waiting to happen for well over thirty years – and now it was over.

While Dan was still waiting for life to happen to him, I was launching myself into it, both socially and professionally. In the past five years or so I've had quite a lot of interest from the media – not just with articles being written about me or our business, but I've also appeared on a number of television programmes, including *Back to the Floor* on BBC2, where various bosses return to the status of employee for a week, the premise being that they will learn more about their businesses. It was a huge learning curve for me and, as a result, I have introduced a Back to the Floor ethos into Ann Summers. Our busiest times of the year are Christmas and Valentine's Day. Every year I ensure that each one of our directors works in an Ann Summers store so that they can really experience what the customer experiences and appreciate the problems that staff might encounter at our most hectic times. As I write this book I am currently involved in filming for two new programmes, *Fortune: Million Pound Giveaway* for ITV and *The Verdict* for BBC2, both of which I'm very excited about. I recognise that my involvement in the media can be good for my business; it is also a new challenge for me.

In addition to television work I write articles on business issues for various publications and speak at conferences and events. I have spoken in front of a diverse range of audiences, everything from a webcast for a small group of people to a speech in front of seven hundred and fifty. In March 2005 I was invited to speak in Shanghai. There was to be an awards night for businesswomen and they wanted an inspirational woman to speak so the organisers kindly asked me. The occasion was very glamorous – I was even loaned some very expensive jewellery to wear. The British girl who was producing the event in Shanghai was stressing me and a fair few others out. The day before I was due to be on stage, she demanded to see the text of my speech. Normally, I would never give details of my speech to anyone in advance, but since we were in a foreign country I thought I may as well show it to her, if only to pacify her. Glancing through it, she spotted a particular story that happened to have the word 'orgasm' in it. 'Oh,' she said, 'you can't put that story in. It's too risqué. You'd better take it out.' 'Fine,' I said. When I got up to give my speech I just ignored her, went with my instinct and related the story. Thinking about it now, I'm not sure how the audience understood all the nuances, but they seemed to, and the story, along with the rest of the speech, went down very well.

Speaking gives me a great sense of satisfaction. It has been a great addition to my career and enabled me to network with people I might not otherwise have been able to. At about the same time I was invited to be on the panel of judges for Retailer of the Year Awards. The awards are sponsored by *Retail Week*, one of the publications for which I write a column.

For me each of these activities is an extension of my business and while they might mean putting in extra time, it's something I really enjoy. At the same time they are a recognition of what I've achieved, something that has been many years in coming. I'm talking about the right sort of recognition, since running Ann Summers has over the years resulted in a great deal of spurious, sensational and frankly nonsensical attention. Back in 1993 a member of my staff nominated me for a 'Women Mean Business' award being run by *Options* magazine. I remember very clearly the first interview, sitting there in front of this panel of judges who seemed to be smirking at me throughout and not really taking me seriously. Looking back, I think it was quite inappropriate that I was being judged by the editor of a magazine, a PR person and some marketing director, none of whom had achieved what I'd achieved. It would have made more sense to be judged by other *businesspeople*. At that time people who wrote about me would often use phrases like the 'sex industry queen', which made me sound like I was running a whorehouse in Arizona instead of a multimillion-pound retail business. This sort of attitude was really common and mostly I ignored it. My business was successful, my customers were happy and I was doing very well, thank you. Occasionally, though, it really made me angry, such as when the *Express* referred to my father and Ralph as the 'Sultans of Sleaze'.

Still, there were people who understood what we'd achieved and what we were about. In February 1995 I was thrilled to be named one of the '40 under-40' businesspeople chosen by *Business Age* magazine. This was a highly prestigious award that in previous years had gone to some real high-flyers, including Richard Branson. The award recognised people whom they thought would still be successful in ten years' time. And now here I was ten years later with a business going stronger than ever! In fact, in 2005 I received an even greater accolade when I was included in Debrett's *People of Today* for my 'Contribution to British Society'. And who would have thought that in 2007 I would have received my first invitation to the palace to attend a reception hosted by the Queen in recognition for my achievements and contribution to business and industry.

I think you have to recognise your own milestones. Things that matter to you and have given you the most satisfaction may not always be big and glitzy. One such milestone was the victory over the JobCentres, which meant a great deal as it showed that the law, the media and the public had understood our business. Perhaps nothing surprised or flattered me more than my invitation to speak at the Oxford Union in 2006. The Oxford Union is regarded as the world's most prestigious debating society. The Union has been established for over a hundred and eighty years and aims to promote discussion on an amazingly broad range of topics, not just within Oxford University but all over the world. The people who have been invited to speak there are very diverse and represent all walks of society. What's great about it is that even though Oxford is a symbol of the establishment, the Union regularly invites its fair share of non-conformists and highly outspoken people, as well as an impressive quota of presidents and prime ministers. I was going to be following in the footsteps of people such as Winston Churchill, the Dalai

Lama, Bill Clinton, Richard Nixon and Mother Teresa! The Union has played host to many people in show business, including Clint Eastwood, Jerry Springer, Madonna, Michael Jackson, Barry White, Warren Beatty and even the US porn star, Jenna Jameson. It is a forum for free speech and as a result people will often say things that aren't heard elsewhere. In 1996 O. J. Simpson made his only public speech in Britain after the 'not guilty' verdict in his criminal trial. This is one place that had seen more controversy than the Gold Group would go through in a lifetime!

When I received their invitation I was stunned. To be asked to speak at one of the world's most influential universities in such a distinguished forum was extraordinary. I remember telling my sister and father first and then my friends. I was hugely excited but I didn't actually appreciate the impact it would have on me until after I had made my presentation.

Upon arrival I was first of all entertained by some of the students at dinner. They were excellent company. Walking into the debating chamber of the Union was both humbling and magical. With its dark wooden floors and benches, its deep red walls and the shafts of light coming through the stained glass windows, I was immediately reminded of Hogwarts and wondered if Harry Potter was about to materialise. The audience was waiting and you could feel this strong sense of anticipation. They were almost all women, with a sprinkling of men, and they'd queued up in the rain since it was held on a first-come, first-served basis. The room could only hold three hundred people, which makes for a very intimate and slightly intimidating environment. There was no microphone but, as I discovered, the auditorium carries your voice. I spoke for about forty minutes. Then it was the audience's turn. I am accustomed to answering challenging questions but these were in a different league altogether and came from perspectives that I had previously not encountered. The audience was intelligent, inquisitive and hungry for knowledge. Their questions included: 'Are you a feminist or are you just another retailer exploiting women?' 'Are you really satisfying women's needs or just pandering to men's sexual desires?' And one cheeky student asked, 'Will you sponsor our hockey team?' To be with them was a truly energising experience. It wasn't easy – but I don't want things to be easy. It's far more stimulating when people make me think and that's what they did.

It had gone well. Afterwards we held an Ann Summers party for some of the young women in the audience in a separate room, which I also attended. It was a fabulous night and I left about midnight to drive back to Kent. The party was a huge success, with sales of £1,400 including seven more party bookings and several orders for the infamous Rampant Rabbit.

It was and is a huge compliment to be recognised at this level; however, perhaps the ultimate indicator of what I've achieved – and what the business has achieved – is the way in which Ann Summers has made a real difference to the lives of many women. We regularly receive letters from women whose lives have been positively changed by being part of our organisation. Much is written today about the responsibility of a business to do more than just make money, but that is a view I have always had and one that is reflected in our working environment, which we have endeavoured to make as female friendly as possible. Of course, the bottom line is important to me but equally so is the knowledge that Ann Summers has enabled many women to take charge of their lives and regain self-esteem. Some of them have had to haul themselves up a long way.

Zena Gavey is an extraordinary success story. She is one of our star Unit Organisers and what makes her story special is that she is registered blind and works with the aid of her guide dog. Along with her team of party organisers, she consistently manages to achieve top results. This is a woman who had been knocked back by many other companies. As she told us in 2004:

> Joining Ann Summers really has been a huge turning point
> in my life. I have spent so much time trying to get retraining
> to go back to work, without any luck. Being told you are too
> old to retrain at thirty-two does knock your confidence. Ann
> Summers has given me back my self-respect.

It is no exaggeration to say that there are many women working for us who've made 360-degree turns in their lives. We regularly share these stories among our party organisers, who find them inspiring and motivating. The story of Lisa is one that I find very moving. Lisa had suffered with depression most of her life, a consequence of having been bullied as a child. At eighteen she got herself into huge debt with credit cards, which sent her into further depression and meant she destroyed any chance of completing her A-levels. Lisa joined us just before her nineteenth birthday in 2001 and says she never imagined she'd stick at it. Initially she wanted to get away from her fiancé who she described as 'very controlling'. Very soon she realised that she was good at party plan and could sell, which gave her a lot of confidence. She also found a new sense of belonging with the other girls in her unit. Lisa was able to gradually reduce her debt and increase her confidence to such an extent that her fiancé began to see her not as someone to control but as an equal. In 2002 she became the top party organiser in her area. By now her depression had all but disappeared and she was looking ahead for the first time in her life. She had, in her own words, *'gone from the girl who couldn't be bothered, and relied on others, to the confident, determined, independent woman with drive who can't sit still for a minute'*.

Like Zena, Lisa credits Ann Summers with turning her life around. But it was Lisa who turned her life around. All that any of us need in this life is an opportunity and the right support, and that's what we give to women like Lisa. When they join us they find a friendly, informative and supportive atmosphere where everything possible is done to help them to succeed. That is what we do. The rest, the ladies do themselves and I am so proud of them.

CHAPTER NINETEEN

She who shouts the softest wins

Invitations to speak at conferences and appear on television make me very aware that whether I like it or not, I am a role model for a lot of women. I recognise that many women operate in an environment where some men still refuse to acknowledge how much they have to offer. I know of many businesswomen and executives – clever, accomplished women – who are not given adequate airtime by their male colleagues. This state of affairs often means that women are so intimidated by the male environment, they compromise by becoming a token man. By that I mean they go to great lengths to not be feminine and adopt an aggressive stance in the workplace in a bid to be accepted as one of the boys. If you are one of the boys and you enjoy it then fine, but don't pretend if you're not. We make life even tougher for ourselves when we try to be something different: it's a burden you don't need in an already competitive workplace.

I remember being invited to be on a judging panel once. When I arrived there was one other woman. She was very good at what she did but I felt that she was trying too hard to play the men at their own game instead of realising she had absolutely everything in her power to compete as a woman. I really do think a lot of women try far too hard to be something they're clearly not instead of just being themselves. You don't need to put on an overly aggressive facade or bang your fist on the table. In fact, that sort of behaviour is likely to put people off. Being a hard-nosed bitch or showing people how ruthless you can be is not going to help you succeed. It might get you noticed but it will do so for all the wrong reasons. You don't need to treat people badly to claim your ground. As a woman you have a lot to offer – it's just a case of being clever about how you do it.

These days I'm known for my love of feminine clothes but it wasn't always so. Growing up, I had no role models to look up to and that, together with my lack of social interaction, meant it took me quite a long time to find out who I was and, more importantly, what image I wanted to portray. I would compromise the way I looked in trying to emulate men and be how I thought people expected me to be. Indeed many years ago I remember going on GMTV – severe suit with shoulder pads and hair tightly pulled back like an old-fashioned librarian – only to watch myself later with horror. When someone said I looked like a politician, I realised I needed to dress to please myself. I've always liked fashion but it's actually only in the past few years that I've become really fashion aware and knowledgeable about what works. While I see it as an integral part of my image and of the Ann Summers brand, I love clothes and looking good. The fact that I love to dress in a feminine way and wear high heels does not in any way compromise my business skills. Talent and business acumen are important for sure, but we live in a world where people are looking for more; they want the whole package. That applies whether you're hiring a senior executive or a young graduate. The bottom line is that dressing well and presenting yourself in the most attractive, and appropriate, way are desirable qualities in the workplace – for men as well as for women.

When I'm hiring for Ann Summers I look for people who can bring things to the company that we don't have. Yes, they must share our brand values and vision, but beyond that I don't want people who've been cut out from the same mould. Unlike many people, I'm not overly concerned about whether someone has been to business school or not. I'm more concerned with what they have done in the real world. If they have an MBA and they have shown great entrepreneurial flair and individuality, then fine, but I don't just want somebody who spouts theory to me. The main qualities that will impress me are:

- commercial approach
- entrepreneurial flair
- ability to think outside the box
- passion for the Ann Summers brand
- not a 'yes' person

This last point is a key one. To a degree, business success, particularly in an entrepreneurial sense, is not worrying about what others think. For some women that is a tough task. It is, I believe, ingrained in many women from the time they are young girls that they shouldn't rock the boat. On the whole conformity is sold to women as more desirable than standing out from the crowd. Now I'm not suggesting you jump on the boardroom table and deliver a rant. Far from it. However, if you have a point of view that you are passionate about and you believe the business needs to hear it, then for goodness sake, don't change it just to fit in. All that will happen then is you will just melt into the background. Sure, people might say, 'Oh, she's a nice girl,' and go out for drinks with you, but will they respect you? Whether I agree with someone or not, I respect them far more if they have the courage of their convictions.

I am incredibly resolute in the boardroom. I will always give plenty of space to others to speak. When you are negotiating you need to take into account what the other person wants: that's a very important negotiating tool. Secondly, I never give the game away. I just listen and keep my deliberations to myself so nobody has any idea which way I'm leaning. It also gives me time to reflect on my decisions. Thirdly, I don't waste my energy on fighting the small battles. I keep my mind on the big picture, on what I'm ultimately trying to achieve and think of the different ways in which I can get there. Remember, if you want to win the war, you need to think strategically. If somebody upsets me I don't always retaliate immediately. Sometimes I will wait for the right time and act accordingly. I should add that I don't set out to make enemies but, as many of you will have discovered, that doesn't stop people making enemies out of you! Unfortunately, that is just a fact of life.

These days, along with my senior team, I'm busy concentrating on taking our business into the future. Today Ann Summers is a true multi-channel retailer. Many companies, including major high-street names, have failed to recognise the importance of this and therefore they're not set up to do it, but I believe it's absolutely key. If you want to survive as a business in this fast-growing retail environment where customers now have a whole host of ways to shop, then you have to expand the ways in which they can access your product and ensure you have a 'One Customer, One Service' infrastructure to support it.

Although people still give us the simplistic 'sex shop' tag, we are, in fact, a sophisticated retail business which has evolved over twenty-five years. We've pushed boundaries to the point where councils now seek our advice when benchmarking and licensing. Our 141 stores represent about 61 per cent of the business. Party plan is around 32 per cent. Our Internet business is the smallest component, with around 7 per cent but it is also the fastest-growing channel with a growth of 30 per cent in 2005–6. This year, 2006–7, we are 40 per cent per week up on the previous year. One of the consequences of this growth is that we've outgrown the functionality and capacity that our current systems and software can provide, so we're working on building that up. If you want to succeed in a major way on the Internet you have to aspire to be as good as Tesco or Amazon, and that means investing a lot of time, money and brainpower into your website. In the future we'll be looking to do a lot more than just sell sex toys and lingerie online. The potential for the Ann Summers brand is enormous, and extensions into online gaming and dating, and sex advice, are all credible fits with our brand values.

One of the new channels we're trialling is vending machines, which will help us reach a new audience in places where people are already having fun such as nightclubs and bars. Of course, one of the things in business you should never do is forget what made you, and we know that party plan is at the heart and soul of our business. Lots of people talk about experiential retailing but that's what we've been doing for twenty-five years. Now we're looking at taking it a bit further. Recognising that we live in a world where being single is utterly normal and should not confine you to sitting at home listening to miserable ballads, we've decided to have Freedom Parties to help the newly single get over their 'ex' and get back into the world. They're all about regaining your confidence and remembering that you're a gorgeous, sexy, fun woman. That's what Ann Summers is all about.

CHAPTER TWENTY

You're never too old

Even though I'm kept busy running a sizeable business, I still have other things I need and want to do. I make every effort to lead a balanced life, which means making time for family and friends as well as for myself. Occasionally, when my personal and professional lives collide the result can be quite surreal. Late in 2006 Vanessa and I were making one of our regular visits to see Grandma Rosie, Dad's mum, in the residential home where she lived. The home, which was more like a five-star hotel, had a lovely atmosphere and they seemed to really care about their residents. That day I was consulting the messages on my telephone rather more than usual. The Gold Group were in the process of selling our private jet business, Gold Air, so I was keeping tabs on the sale, which was rather a large one. After visiting Rosie I would be attending a meeting to finalise the deal.

Meanwhile an entertainer had arrived at the home and was singing to the assembled crowd. I was anxiously looking at my texts and half-listening to the song when he came up, unexpectedly grabbed one of my leopard-print shoes and proceeded to show it to the elderly residents, who seemed bemused and perhaps bewildered by it all. He finished with my shoe and gave it back. He then asked if Vanessa and I were sisters and invited me up on stage. Still participating in the deal, and still sending messages, I found myself up there beside him. The crooner, who was still crooning, then went and got Vanessa and soon both of us were up on stage dancing, me wearing a Mexican hat and Vanessa a poncho. He'd told us to keep dancing while he sang his finale. By now we'd really got into the spirit and decided to go down among the audience and freestyle, especially Vanessa who was now twirling me enthusiastically around the room, having apparently forgotten that I needed to be in good shape for the meeting that was to follow. As we finished and were trying to make our escape, the entertainer called down to me from the stage and asked me what I did for a living. Exhausted, I looked up at him and said, 'If only you knew!'

Rosie, of course, had been Goddy's wife but they had divorced over thirty-five years earlier. Goddy, always the rogue, had then had a relationship with a seventeen-year-old girl, which resulted in a son called Mark. Several years later, after falling out with Ralph and Dad, he signed over all his money to Mark, thinking it would be safe. Mark ran off to South Africa and hasn't been heard of since! The result is that Dad and Ralph have been helping Goddy out financially. Now an old man of ninety, he still retains his East End attitude and has lost none of his desire to capitalise on an opportunity, as we were to discover in late 2005.

It all started innocently enough when Julie Harris was having her nails done at a salon called Pinkys, where I also sometimes went. While sitting there, she overheard another client gossiping about a house where the client's friend Lori had worked as a home help. Apparently, Lori subsequently found out the house was being used as a brothel. As Lori was also a nail technician at Pinkys, Julie took a lot of interest in the conversation. The story was that an old man of about ninety years old, who owned the house, slept with very young girls from the Eastern Bloc and that some of them were as young as sixteen. A remark was made that at his age, sleeping would probably be all he could do! The woman telling the story continued to say how disgusted Lori was and that she was concerned that people might think she was a prostitute instead of the home help. Until she made her discovery, Lori used to give the old man a lift to the hospital and do odd jobs around the house for him. There was nothing to suggest he was anything more than a harmless old boy.

Julie told me later that the person who was doing her nails seemed very uncomfortable about the conversation. However, Julie was fascinated so she kept listening and learnt that the house was in this smart road where there were expensive cars coming and going at all hours. All of a sudden Julie put two and two together, and realised that the old man they were talking about must be my grandfather, Goddy Gold. At this point she says she was caught between laughing at such a preposterous situation and wondering what she was going do with this little gem of information! Julie and I are very close and she knew that I did not see him or have anything to do with him. She sat there wondering how on earth she was going to deliver the words, 'Jacqueline, I'm sorry to tell you but your grandad is running a whore-house!' At the same time she was obviously concerned about our business and what would happen if the press got hold of the story. Apparently, the technician then gave Julie a set of keys and a hospital registration card to return to the family, as Lori had no intention of going back to the house. She asked Julie to give them to me. Julie didn't think this was right so she refused the keys and suggested they be given to my Auntie Marie, who also had her nails done at the salon.

Four weeks later, on her next visit to the salon, it was still the conversation of the day and apparently the local residents were all up in arms and ready to revolt as there were cars coming in and out at all hours of the day and night; it was now common knowledge that the house was being run as a brothel. Many had threatened to go to the police, so the risk of bad publicity was quite high. Ever the professional, Julie was concerned because she knew that if it got out, the press would try and drag me in. She decided to take matters into her own hands and do a bit of sleuthing. She managed to get the number that the brothel used for appointments (not Goddy's home number) and then asked her son to call the number and 'make an appointment' for himself. The address he was given was indeed Goddy's home address! Meanwhile poor Lori was beside herself as her dentist had mentioned the brothel to her and knew she worked at the house. Julie decided to call Lori to try and defuse the situation and calm her down. All Lori could say was that she felt disgusted at Goddy, that she had washed his bits and now did not know where they had been! It was all too bizarre to be true: an elderly man who could not bathe himself was running a brothel from his grand house.

Julie finally decided it was time to tell me. I don't know what she was expecting me to say but I do know she apparently spent ages rehearsing the most tactful words she could find to tell me my grandad was a pimp. When she finally told me I wasn't surprised at all. It turned out that Goddy had befriended some Eastern European women who came to work for him around the house, saw an opportunity to take advantage of an old man and set up a brothel. As for Goddy, he just enjoyed the benefits until visits from the council and police, plus pressure from the family, meant he asked the girls to leave.

In the autumn of 2006 my beloved Grandma Rosie suddenly fell ill and after a very short illness died peacefully, with her family around her, at the age of ninety-two.

Until Rosie's funeral I hadn't seen or heard from my grand-father, Goddy, for about fifteen years. Mum enjoyed taking Vanessa and me to see Grandad even though he'd divorced Rosie and no longer had any contact with Dad. After leaving home, Vanessa and I made fewer visits, partly because he would always find an opportunity to say 'your father is a bastard'. Even though we weren't close to Dad at that time, we both found this hard to take. As Grandad walked into the chapel I didn't immediately recognise him. Age had shrunken him a little and I suppose I had no idea what he should look like. I discovered he was surprisingly mentally sharp and physically quite agile for his age. The thing I noticed the most was how he had mellowed. Nonetheless, it was hard to keep a straight face thinking about his recent business activity!

We have a large extended family but, other than Dad and Vanessa, I have only ever been really close to Rosie, whom I absolutely adored. She was a real girlie girl even in her nineties. Because she lived for most of her life in the East End I didn't see her as often as I would have liked. She was a devout football fan and her first love was West Ham. And my father's passion for Birmingham City FC was shared by Rosie, who used to travel up to the vast majority of home games. She was vivacious with a passionate personality and would lift the spirits of anyone fortunate enough to meet her. Vanessa and I thoroughly enjoyed taking her out for girlie lunches and gossip. On one occasion when Grandma was in her eighties, she was dating a man twenty years younger and was complaining to us about their relationship in a typical girlie fashion. Then, out of the blue and oblivious to the waiter standing there, she said, 'There's no sex any more, you know.' It was a very funny moment and needless to say, he was dumped soon after.

Rosie was such an inspiration to me and we related to each other on so many levels. She was extremely glamorous and, like me, she loved getting dressed up to go out. She was meticulous about coordinating her outfits right down to the smallest detail. Socialising was an inherent part of her personality, whether it was her nightly visit to the West Ham supporters' club, her weekly visit to the Senior Citizens' club at St Andrews, which she cofounded with her friend Thelma or her weekly visit to the gym – yes, in her early nineties she insisted on her regular visits to the gym. At ninety-two she was an incredible lady who had survived lung cancer at the age of fifty. She lived life to the full and refused to listen to anyone who dared to suggest she should slow down. I loved her determination and her energy, and loved just being in her presence. She was a true lady and will always be my inspiration.

CHAPTER TWENTY-ONE

The Golden Girls

If I'd been able to step outside the situation I was in with Dan I would have recognised that I was caught up in a vicious circle where regret was immediately followed by promises which would then be broken. There would be more regret, more promises and so on. We were at that desperate state in a relationship where you throw anything at it just to keep it going, hence Dan declaring that he wanted to marry me. As we all know words are just that unless they are supported by some seriously meaningful behaviour, which I wasn't seeing. While I believe that deep down I knew it had to end, I didn't want to accept it. I suppose you could look at it as either optimism or stupidity – or simply human nature. Between September 2004 and July 2005 Dan had returned, left and returned once more, just in time for my birthday. Again it was to be a themed party – this time a White Party. The party itself was great fun but, once again, it wasn't long before we hit our usual obstacles. Nevertheless, even though I was upset and confused about our relationship, I was determined to extract as much fun as I could from life.

The worst thing you can do is put your life on hold for a man. I have realised that whatever is going to happen will happen whether you stay at home and mope or go out and have fun. Fun for me inevitably means girlie holidays with my sister Vanessa and our friend Sandie, and I wasn't going to stop those for Dan or anybody. In May 2005 we planned to jet off to Spain in search of sun and whatever else transpired.

I'd been speaking at a business conference in the morning so it was agreed that I would make my own way to the airport. The three of us met up there and headed off to deal with important things, i.e. glasses of wine that were awaiting us in the BA Club Lounge. We completely missed the flight boarding calls and had to endure the shame of hearing our surnames boomed out over the tannoy. With only a few minutes to spare before the gate closed, we then had to run from the Lounge to the boarding gate. Vanessa was the first to arrive at the gate, having overtaken Sandie and me, both of us gasping for air in a very unattractive manner. As if in a relay race, Vanessa managed to grab our boarding tickets as she passed so she could hold things up at the gate for us. The stewardess suggested it might be a good idea if she called out our names again on the tannoy. Thoughtfully, Vanessa told her this was a bad idea, as it was more likely to give us a heart attack than speed us along.

A couple of months later, just before Dan came back in July, the girlies set off once again for La Manga. This is a beautiful resort located on Spain's Costa Calida, in Murcia. As well as the five-star luxury – my preferred way of travel – there is no shortage of things to do: golf, tennis, spa, swimming, mountain biking, water sports, horse riding – the list goes on. Most of this is lost on us since we are too busy getting up to mischief and sharpening our wit on each other. And nobody is sharper than Sandie. As well as being a source of good advice, she has always been the joker of the pack. She is sassy, sharp-tongued and capable of turning the most desperate situation into a joke. We have a very honest relationship characterised as much by a love of clever humour as by our love and respect for each other. I respect her honesty: if Sandie is giving me grief I will give it back to her. I've called her a witch and an evil cow, and I can get away with things with her that I would never dream of saying to anybody else. In turn she will say to me, 'Stop being precious, darling.' She is aware that I don't like hearing that so she knows she's getting to me. On holidays together, when we are all getting a bit tired and emotional, she might say, 'Jaq, you're really getting on my nerves.' I won't be offended.

Mostly we just take pleasure in mercilessly ripping each other apart and I actually find when I'm with her that my wit is sharper. During our holiday in La Manga we were all in good form. After one evening filled with varying degrees of male attention she said to me, 'I can't believe you were talking to that Simon last night. He was such a tosser.' 'Babe,' I replied, 'I gave my tongue to that "tosser".' There was something about that particular trip that fuelled our desire for more girlie weekends. A couple of weeks later we boarded a plane to Barcelona and brazenly gatecrashed Sandie's future sister-in-law's hen weekend.

The girlie weekends were a great diversion from the indecision that now characterised my relationship with Dan. Having poured his heart out about how much he missed me prior to returning in July, we were now stumbling along, sometimes very happy, sometimes just existing. It was not, and is not, the way I want to live with the man I love, but I loved him. Were we marking time? Perhaps we were. There is a view that once you spend more time talking about your relationship than actually having it, you're in trouble. One of the worst moments was when we'd gone out for dinner with Vanessa and Nick, and Sandie and her husband Graham. Afterwards we went to a nightclub. We were having a good time, or so I thought until I turned round to him and said, 'Babe, I'd like to take you home and make mad, passionate love to you.' He just said, 'Why don't you back off!' I went into the toilet with Sandie, and, holding back the tears, told her what had happened. When we got home I was still very upset as he had made me feel completely undesirable. He was drunk and went to sleep.

Somehow we limped along to Christmas 2005. The day itself seemed to give us a spark, which was good since we were hosting. I had decided that I was going to hold it at home and I went all out to make sure every detail was perfect. It was the first time I'd done a proper Christmas at the Barn and I really went for it. I love entertaining and I saw this as a great opportunity to use my artistic skills. We invited all of Dan's family; in total there were twenty of us. With the help of Dan's mum Lyn, his sister Lorna and Aunt Mary, I cooked a full traditional Christmas dinner. Even Dan's dad, Roger, dressed up as Santa and delighted the children. I made chocolate place settings and baked Christmas cookies on to which I piped everyone's name. We even had Santa's footsteps going from the chimney to the tree! The house looked magical and everyone later said it had been a brilliant day. Dan's nieces and nephews were there. They are so sweet and, although Dan adores them, he didn't seem to find it easy to be around any children at this time. You could see it trigger a change in him within a few hours. When Boxing Day dawned, he was very withdrawn and things were pretty miserable. We went to Devon for New Year's Eve with loads of friends. When we returned on New Year's Day he came in to the lounge and burst into tears. He just looked at me and said, 'I don't love you the same way I did three months ago.' That was the first time he'd said it like that.

Dan left for good on New Year's Day 2006. Even if you are expecting something to happen it doesn't lessen the impact when it does. The thought that we were finally saying goodbye left me heartbroken. But I didn't hate Dan. It's hard to hate someone who reminds you of a wounded puppy. That night Sandie came to stay with me and I cried all night. In the morning I woke up to the full realisation that it was finished. It was time to get on with the rest of my life. He came around one day to discuss splitting up the house and possessions and he sobbed the entire time. I don't know what he expected me to say. I asked him, 'If we'd had a baby would you have stayed?' He replied yes, of course. I said, 'So your love was conditional, then?'

I don't think Dan was a poor choice. If I met another Dan tomorrow, but ten years older, I would definitely get involved with him. We enjoyed each other's company and doing the same things. The age gap indirectly became an issue for us both. Me because, when Dan was faced with problems in his life for the very first time, he was too emotionally immature to deal with them. And, from his point of view, I think the time clock issue challenged his ideals. It wasn't just the stress of IVF, but also the philosophical difference in our attitudes towards having children. I was and am able to accept that if it doesn't happen I will still have a great life. Of course, I would be deeply disappointed but I am grateful for everything I have and determined to enjoy every moment of it. For Dan our inability to conceive when he wanted to suddenly meant that everything he already had in his life was suddenly less meaningful. His inability to live in the moment, and my desire to live every moment, was probably an even larger gap between us than our ages. I stayed in the relationship long after it was clear that I was no longer being true to myself – partly because I feared I had fallen short in some way and partly because I thought I could turn our problems around. What I have learnt though is that you can't fix someone; they have to want to fix themselves.

I was determined not to let our break up get to me. Perhaps prematurely, I decided to take myself on holiday to Barbados, in January. It was awful and I could not enjoy myself at all. I don't know what I was expecting. I remember there were many times when my friend Val rang me and said, 'Jaq, give me the word and I will be on the next plane out to join you.' I declined and ended up coming home early. Val is another one of my closest friends. We first met when I was looking at new fit-outs for our shops. Val has her own design business of which shop fit is a component. Like me, she frequently goes abroad for business and we will often organise our meetings for Mondays so that we have an excuse to go away for the weekend – as if we needed any! Val has been married and has two grown-up sons. To say she is glamorous, elegant and sophisticated is not an exaggeration. She's also utterly loyal, with excellent powers of reasoning. If you talk to her about your problems she'll generally come back to you with something very incisive.

A couple of months after breaking up from Dan, Val orchestrated a trip for us to Helsinki. She had a meeting during the week so we had a weekend to play. Val is a great planner: she had looked up all the hot restaurants and clubs, and had visualised a big night out for us. Our first stop was a restaurant and club she'd found. Val had sensibly instructed me to bring my trainers and boots in order to navigate the ice and snow, but I couldn't help it and had to bring my Jimmy Choos. Val put on trousers and boots and still looked very glamorous but appropriate. I, on the other hand, thought, 'Bugger it, dressing up is what I love and I'm going to wear my Jimmys with my jeans.' I figured we were getting a taxi so what was the problem? When we arrived, all the women had Ugg-type boots on. I was the only woman with strappy high heels on but I felt good.

We sat down to eat in this fabulous restaurant which was attached to a club and life was looking good. There were quite a few men looking at us so we were happily contemplating the attention to come. Suddenly Val puts down her fork and says, 'Oh my God!' 'What's wrong, Val?' I asked, thinking she might have forgotten something. 'I've broken my tooth ... the front one.' It was actually one of the teeth to the side of the two front ones, but that didn't make it any less visible as the whole cap had come off, revealing the peg underneath. It was so funny that I just burst out laughing while Val sat there looking utterly dejected. I laughed so much it hurt. Val was unimpressed with my reaction so I composed myself and switched to my default problem-solving setting.

'We'll get some chewing gum, you can chew it and then we'll use it to stick the tooth back on for the night.'

'Jaq – even if that worked, I can't do it.'

'Why not?'

'I've swallowed the tooth'

I burst out laughing again and couldn't stop. Val looked perplexed. 'Are we going back to the hotel?' she whined.

'No, we're not. We've come all this way and we are going to enjoy ourselves, with teeth or not!'

Val looked cross and went to the ladies' – probably to get away from me. As far as I was concerned, Val's tooth problem was a minor hitch in the evening. While she was in the toilet I went to the bar. As I'm walking to the bar I felt something go from under one of my feet. It was the heel of one of my shoes. I looked down and it was completely broken. By now I'm halfway to the bar so I continued walking on tiptoe. There were lots of guys standing around looking very friendly. The men in Helsinki reminded me of a cross between Bart Simpson and Arnie

Schwarzenegger and they are incredibly forward, which is no bad thing.

I went back to the table and Val joined me. 'Val,' I said, 'you're not going to believe what's happened to me. The heel on one of my Choos has broken.' Now the laugh was on me and I could see her thinking, 'Yes, there is a God.' We were definitely not going back to the hotel. Val couldn't smile. I couldn't dance. But we were determined to see our evening through. We went to the club area where there was a separate check-in. At that moment a tall Bart Simpson lookalike comes around the corner. In his robotic English he tells the person at the entrance, 'These two girls are with me.' Well, that's that sorted, we thought. He turned to us and said, 'You are coming into the VIP lounge.' When he said VIP he said it as a word rather than the letters, which made it sound very silly. Neither of us fancied him but he seemed to have claimed us. He was obviously quite wealthy and, accordingly, lavish with the champagne. As we were sitting there someone he knew came over and he introduced us saying, 'This is my friend. He is an arsehole.' Spoken in his broken Icelandic English, it came out sounding like a bad Schwarzenegger line. I assumed he was joking but I wasn't sure and said to Val, 'I'm not sure if I want to stay here.'

His friend sat down to talk to him. 'Would you like to go for a dance and see the rest of the club?' he asked. We established between us that we would do so without him and then enthusiastically agreed. It was our chance to escape. As we left he said, 'I have a gun in my pocket so you must come back otherwise I will shoot you!' We didn't come back to find out if he would or not. We continued into the night and didn't get in until after three in the morning. I danced. Val smiled. And we walked back to the hotel with ice on the ground. Who needs sturdy boots?

My resolve, however, was sturdy. It had to be since Dan was calling me saying he regretted splitting up. But this time there was no going back. While I was missing him, the year had begun well, with my speech at the Oxford Union being a major highlight. In May Sandie, Vanessa and I made what is now our annual trip to La Manga, and then in June we were off to Marbella to stay at our favourite hotel, the Puento Romana, just outside Puerto Banus. This luxurious hotel is one of the Leading Hotels of the World and a hotel that Vanessa and I have stayed at on many occasions. Once you pass through the hotel foyer, the bedrooms, built in the style of an old Spanish village, meander all the way down to the beach with a picturesque river running through the grounds. Our room, which the three of us were sharing, was about a five-minute walk from the foyer.

I've always said that one of the best things about a girlie night out is getting ready. Our luxury room was spacious and easily accommodated our three beds along with a large couch, dressing table and chair. At the end of the room were double doors leading on to the balcony which overlooked the stunning pool area. Our clothes were laid out, our make-up ready to go and there was a fine bottle of rosé chilling in the ice bucket. The only thing left to do was plug in my iPod on which I have set up multiple playlists. As is our way, we drank, chatted and sang as we got ourselves ready. Then having decided we all looked gorgeous, we made our way through the grounds of the hotel back to the foyer. We were catching a cab to the port. The three of us had tended to be wine drinkers in the past, rarely deviating to drink anything else – except champagne. This was the holiday we all decided that vodka and cranberry was our drink. It was refreshing and tasted so much like a fruit cocktail that, assisted by the intense Spanish heat, we may have drunk far more alcohol than usual.

As it was the time of the World Cup, the atmosphere in the port was buzzing more than usual. Surrounded by a mixture of nationalities, we drank, chatted and laughed our way from bar to bar. One thing that none of us lacks is confidence, and having been single a few months now, I felt that I was ready to abandon myself to the world once again. It was a great ego-boost to have all this male attention and I was feeling very positive about myself. In the early hours of the morning, worn out by alcohol, fun and our high heels, we made our way back to our hotel.

I still don't know what got into me. Maybe it was my symbolic gesture but I then did something that left Sandie and Vanessa completely stunned. As we passed through the foyer, I found that my feet were hurting so I stopped at the top of the steps to take my shoes off. Sandie and Vanessa were following me across the old Roman Bridge. Without pausing, and much to their surprise, I then pulled my top over my head and continued to walk at the same pace in front of them. Vanessa says what really amused her was that I neatly folded my top over my arm. I did exactly the same with my jeans. I then removed my bra and my thong and continued to walk to the room naked. By the time we had neared our room I had even removed my earrings and false eyelashes, which I was carefully holding with the tips of my fingers. I reached the room before Vanessa and Sandie and turned to see the looks of disbelief on their faces. When they asked me why I had removed all my clothes, I gave them the honest answer: 'I was getting ready for bed, of course.'

Vanessa said later that she and Sandie were incredulous. They had seen that I was brimming with confidence on this trip but the idea that I would do something like that totally caught them by surprise. They particularly loved that I did it so deliberately and folded my clothes as I went! None of us can understand how I managed not to be seen by a single person in or around the hotel!

The following night we once again found ourselves in a lively bar at the port, and as we sipped our new favourite drink we were entertained by a magician. He came over to where we were standing and selected me, plus a good-looking guy who was flirting with me, for his magic trick with some playing cards. He asked Vanessa and Sandie and some English guys in the crowd to write down a word on their card without him seeing it. While the boys predictably wrote 'Manchester United', Vanessa and Sandie wrote 'PEACHES'. On finalising the trick, and with our card mysteriously reappearing out of the centre of an orange, 'PEACHES' was there for all to see. The guys got the joke and were in no doubt who Peaches was, and to this day Vanessa still has the naked proof of my bare bottom on her mobile phone!

I have often referred to Sandie, Vanessa and myself as the witches because when we are together we conjure up a lot of mischief. The day following the unveiling of Peaches, the three of us woke to a beautiful morning with perfect clear blue sky, birds singing and a shocking hangover, the sort where any movement is painful. However, there was sunbathing to be done so we had breakfast on our balcony, packed our bikinis and headed to an exclusive beach club called Nikki Beach just outside of Marbella.

Nikki Beach is a popular haunt for the world's rich and famous. It is furnished with plush white double beds with waiters catering for your every need. Music plays all day and the champagne and cocktails never stop coming. This is just the place to relax and nurse a hangover in preparation for the night ahead and that's exactly what we did. We then headed back to the hotel for our customary evening ritual of getting ready.

You could tell it was going to be a serious party night. Puerto Banus was packed with locals and tourists, and everyone was out in the streets to watch England v Portugal on massive TV screens in their World Cup match. It was just the most electric atmosphere, with everyone singing and cheering for both teams. Although England lost the game, the party did not let up and we carried on through the port visiting different bars until we finally ended up in the most infamous bar of them all, Sinatra's. Vanessa tells me I had a special glow that night. I certainly felt in my element, and the amount of male attention I was receiving confirmed that something must be right. There was one guy in particular who caught my eye, so naturally I began flirting with him. Meanwhile Sandie and Vanessa chatted to his friends.

We are all capable of looking after ourselves but when you are away with the girls in a foreign country you always tend to keep an eye out for each other. Vanessa apparently noticed that I had been gone for a while and she suggested to Sandie that they look for me. Normally, when any one of us leaves the group for whatever reason we usually let the others know where we are off to, but in this case I had just disappeared. What Sandie and Vanessa didn't know as they wandered alongside the luxurious multimillion-pound yachts looking for me was that I was hiding from them, snogging my new friend!

They then headed back to the bar, thinking I might be there. Of course, I had long gone but those girls were persistent so in the end one of the guys from the group offered to take them to their apartment to see if I was there. I had no idea the girls were on my trail. The apartment was quite large with several bedrooms leading off from the long corridor, and I believe one of the guys did come in but left saying he couldn't find us. I don't know how hard he'd looked. However, Vanessa is nothing if not determined and buoyed by all the alcohol she decided to search the apartment herself. The way she describes it, she was 'marching down the corridor' only to see a naked man holding a pair of shorts in front of him. He quickly fled and she followed him.

Vanessa had then stormed into the bedroom where my new friend was standing by the bed. At the same time she called me on her mobile. All she could see were the sheets pulled to the top of the bed. Sandie arrived and apparently they were both wondering why there was a blue light flashing underneath the covers. It was, of course, my mobile phone. I could stand it no longer. I threw the covers back, glared at the girls and shouted 'What are you f***ing witches doing at the end of the bed?'

We all paused for a moment and I swear I could see Vanessa mouthing the words: 'Jacqueline, *not* in Marbella!' She was then unceremoniously dragged out of the room by Sandie. The evening had been disrupted but it was not ruined since I had already planned to make an exit. While my new friend was cute, he had somehow let slip that he wanted me to be his holiday romance, a concept that did not appeal to the new fun-loving Peaches. I was free at last!

Postscript

I waited a very long time to write this book because I wasn't ready until now. I knew that when I sat down to write, it would be a very personal memoir that would include things even my close friends and family did not know about until they read the manuscript. I have in the past been very private about my personal life, but having faced my childhood demons, I suddenly had this necessary urge to share my story. I also could not have written this book while my mother was alive. While there are places in this book where she has perhaps not acted in the way you might expect a mother to, I could not have subjected such a fragile woman to any fallout that may result. Despite everything, I still love her. No matter how much I have suffered, this book is not about exacting revenge. It is simply about telling it as it is and showing that adversity can shape you in a positive way.

I had met many women at business events where I was a speaker and often they would be keen to know the reasons for my success and how they could overcome their own challenges of being a businesswoman in a man's world. They all had different stories to tell and many were striving for success, often against a background of business and personal issues in their own lives. My aim in writing this book, and sharing my story and all the challenges I have faced, is the hope that it might inspire people like these to recognise that if I can achieve despite such horrendous life experiences, then so could they. It has not been easy to revisit particular parts of my life; at times it has not just affected me emotionally but physically as well. Occasionally, the process of recounting my memories has truly shocked me. Yet I also feel quietly euphoric that I have risen above it and lead a progressive life, filled with potential and opportunity.

I want to make it clear I am not Superwoman. I am not gifted with any special emotional armoury that allows me to casually brush off events that would cause others to collapse. What I am blessed with is enormous amounts of self-belief and a consistently positive attitude. I am one of those people – and there are many others out there – who is driven to improve my life in the face of adversity; it's almost like the worse things get, the more I think, 'I can do this.' At such times I seem to propel myself to a new level that I never thought possible. That is not to say I don't stumble and fall. Of course I do.

When Dan, the man I loved and my partner of five

years, walked out on New Year's Day 2006 it was the culmination of a very testing and draining few years. Knowing he was leaving for good was heartbreaking, as dramatic as that may sound. However, I also felt an underlying sense of relief. Once I had accepted the door was finally closed, I set about fixing myself. I am a firm believer in keeping busy, so my first reaction was to fill my social diary so that it was bursting with possibilities. I then made a list of all the things that I loved doing. I also made a list of all the things I had ever wanted to do. I wrote down everything I could think of that made me feel good about myself and all the things that would bring laughter and joy into my life. Before I knew it my diary was splitting at the seams and, aided and abetted by my friends and family, I was once again starting to see life in a happier glow.

That didn't mean that my heart was not hurting. It would be a total lie to say I was fine because I wasn't. Restoring your equilibrium after you have been through a difficult time cannot be rushed. The key here is to accept that part of you is still yearning for what you have lost. There is no point trying to suppress it. I knew it would take more than a busy social calendar to rid myself of the hurt and loss that I was feeling. It would take more than a few holidays, days at the spa and new high heels. All these things are wonderful but, let's face it, they are pretty super-ficial. If you are going to redirect your life, you need to dig deep and make some significant changes. For me there is nothing like a new challenge to make me feel good about myself. My view is that if you can make it out of your comfort zone you can make it. I decided to set myself some serious and challenging goals for the year ahead. It took until March before I felt ready to do this; I had already lost two months of the year but I was determined to achieve my goals by Christmas.

I began by reflecting over that previous year. What had gone wrong? What parts of it could I have influenced differently? And, more importantly, what lessons had I learnt? I then went on to highlight the reasons for my success, reminding myself of what worked. This enabled me to put together some personal guidelines which reinforced my personal values and beliefs, some of which had got lost in the traumas of the previous year. I reminded myself about the importance of being true to myself, focusing on what I had rather than couldn't have, spending more time on me and enjoying the here and now. I also thought long and hard as to whether I had fallen into the trap of creating limitations in my life, and of course I had. Often when our self-esteem is at a low ebb we think negative thoughts, and if we continually feed ourselves with a whole list of 'I can't do this' or 'I can't do that' we end up believing it. One example of this for me was, after failing to lose the two stone I had gained three years ago following the IVF treatment, I convinced myself that I was never going to lose the weight.

My other limitation was in believing that I was never going to find a fulfilling relationship.

Recognising the existence of my self-imposed limitations was the first step in getting rid of them. By the time I got to the next stage of putting together my personal life-changing strategy I was feeling very excited about what I was discovering and optimistic about the changes I could implement. I have always believed there is a solution to every problem in life if you are prepared to take responsibility for your own destiny. I have never been one to wait for happiness or success to come to me. I am an impatient, self-changing and self-correcting person by nature and I believe the only way to make things happen is to go get it yourself.

Just doing this exercise changed my outlook on life from the inside out. And slowly but surely my life began to find its equilibrium. The girl who woke up crying on New Year's Day was gradually disappearing, and emerging in her place was the me that I liked to spend time with, the me I respected, the me that I wanted the world to see.

I put together a list of twenty goals from all areas of my life and highlighted the ten most important ones that I wanted to achieve that year. They are, in random order:

- Launch new Freedom Parties for single women
- Launch new Ann Summers website

- Lose two stone
- Commit to an exercise training programme
- Write autobiography
- Redesign my entrance hall
- Find the gorgeous, charismatic man of my dreams
- Spend more time with my friends
- Participate or present on a primetime TV show
- Be a better sister

By December 2006 I had achieved nearly all of my goals within the timescale I set myself. I adore my sister who was a great support to me during the break up of my relationship. I feel sad to admit that I almost totally neglected her needs during this time and now am glad to say I feel I am giving her the love and support she deserves. I have already lost a stone and a half of the two stone I had gained. Success is not just about being focused and having a strategy, but with challenges such as weight loss the chances of achieving your chosen goals are also linked to your frame of mind. I realise now why it was so impossible to succeed when I was in the depths of despair. As well as committing to a healthy eating plan, I have also put myself on an exercise training programme twice a week with a personal trainer and my friend Julie, something I recently increased to three times a week. My focus is not just about losing weight but I also want to participate in the Moonwalk in May 2007 to raise money and awareness for breast cancer. I hope that my training will pay dividends during the thirteen-hour walk throughout the night! I am also mindful that my profile will help me raise as much money as I possibly can.

One of the things I have recognised is that my selective involvement in television projects raises the profile of my business. It also takes me outside my comfort zone. After twenty-five years of running Ann Summers it has been great for me to try something different and challenge myself personally in different ways. It was therefore a great opportunity to be involved in filming two major television shows and to be asked to do a second book.

It's important to take time out to acknowledge where you have got to and now I am in a rewarding place in all aspects of my life. My business is doing well, I am achieving new goals and I feel good about me. I often find that women, especially, make the mistake of focusing their lives on their partner and immediate family, neglecting their own needs in the process. My mother was the epitome of this. She put her life in the hands of another and it destroyed her. I have realised that fulfilling all of my hopes and desires has put me in the wonderful place I am in now, completely open to new opportunities, new friends and hopefully my soulmate. As for the man of my dreams, well, he will turn up when the time is right. Meanwhile I will continue to strive towards personal satisfaction and contentment because I believe that unless you are happy with who *you* are, you will never be happy with another.

Throughout my career I have met some wonderful and amazing people from different walks of life. I am not elitist about who I talk to or even who I date, and will give the time of day to almost anybody. However, the only people I will avoid are people who act like victims, the ones who blame everything and everyone else for their misfortunes, and then go on about it throughout most of their life, taking no responsibility for their own actions. I've learnt that being around this type of people for too long will only serve to bring you down. In any case, I find I always gravitate towards positive, energetic people with similar views and values to my own. Equally, I avoid people who, even in some small way, treat me like a victim. That also goes for those well-meaning types who look at you with pity when they ask you if you've met anyone yet, in a way that makes you feel like you must have a contagious rash or something! Yes, even if you run a multimillion-pound business you are never immune to those sorts of questions!

No matter what company I am in, the question I get asked the most is the reason for my success. There are many factors, but here I pick out my top five:

1. **Be an opportunist.** How many people come across opportunities in their everyday lives, are momentarily

excited by the thought but let it pass them by for fear of the unfamiliar, or failure. I wanted success badly, so I knew I couldn't be one of them.

2. **Listen.** When I started Ann Summers I had no business experience and no formal training. I was forced to rely on feedback from my customers and staff. That wasn't the drawback I initially thought, but something that has formed part of the ethos of our business today.

3. **Focus.** I am incredibly focused, and I focus my people on being the best. I don't allow myself to be distracted from what I want to achieve.

4. **Self-belief.** I set my sights high based on my belief in myself and the business, and not on the expectations or opinions of others.

5. **Perseverance.** The person who gets ahead is the one who does more than is necessary and keeps on doing it. There is no substitute for perseverance.

Above all of these is my personal favourite, **Courage**. The real test of courage comes when you are in the minority, a place I have been many times but self-belief and passion for my business made me resolute in pursuing what I believed in. Courage is not the absence of fear but the conquest of it. As my father used to tell me, 'There is nothing to fear but fear itself' and of course, he was right. Nonetheless, it takes immense courage to step outside your comfort zone and pursue your dreams. When you do, I guarantee, the reward is huge and your new-found confidence will give you the courage to discover and achieve even more. Challenge yourself and great things will happen.